SOLIDARNOŚĆ

The workers' movement and the rebirth of Poland in 1980-81

BY MARK OSBORN

Solidarność: the workers' movement and the rebirth of Poland in 1980-81

By Mark Osborn

Published by Workers' Liberty, January 2020

workersliberty.org

awl@workersliberty.org

20E Tower Workshops
Riley Road
London SE1 3DG

020 7394 8923

Printed by Imprint Digital
Exeter
EX5 5HY

ISBN: 978-1-909639-49-2

Contents

THE WORKERS' MOVEMENT AND THE REBIRTH OF POLAND IN 1980-81

After the War

At the war's end, in 1945, half of Poland's pre-war public transport system, 60% of schools, post and telecommunications, and a third of industrial plant and half of all bridges had been destroyed. 80% of the capital, Warsaw, was in ruins, much of the damage deliberately inflicted by the Nazis following the Warsaw rising of August 1944.

The census of February 1946 showed Poland had a population of 24 million, down from 35 million in 1939. The drop was partly due to border shifts, Poland had been moved 200km West by Stalin, removing Ukrainian and other populations into the USSR. Poland was now smaller by a fifth.

About 4.5 million ethnic Germans remained in the territory of the new Poland defined under the Potsdam Agreement, others having fled or been evacuated at the end of the War. By 1950 3.1 million had been expelled to Germany.

Poland had also had six million citizens killed during the war, including three million Jewish Holocaust victims. 90% of Poland's Jews died under the Nazi occupation.

Only around a quarter of a million Polish Jews survived, and half of these had migrated to Palestine. Jews that remained or returned were subjected to a new wave of antisemitism. On 4 July 1946 a pogrom took place in Kielce, killing 42 and wounding another 40 Jews. The Polish Primate, Cardinal Hlond, commented that this attack on Jews was a political protest against "the presence in government of Jews who were trying to establish in Poland a regime to which the majority of the people are hostile."

Both the "Soviet" Stalinists and the Nazis had attempted to wipe out Polish elites. (By 1945 "soviet", in common usage, had lost its original meaning of "workers' council", and had come to mean a radical opposite: "Russian Stalinist".) The "Soviet" secret police, the NKVD, massacred 8000 captured members of the Polish officer corps in the Katyn forest in mid-1940. Also killed were 6000 police and thousands of middle-class Poles considered politically suspect.

Bolesław Bierut (1892-1956), "Poland's Stalin," was the Moscow-line Stalinist who was the central leader of the Polish United Workers' Party from 1948 until his death in 1956

In May 1940 the Nazis launched AB-Aktion, a campaign to destroy the Polish intelligentsia and political leadership. Under German occupation 2,900 – or 20% — of priests, half of all lawyers and doctors and 40% of University professors were killed. Millions of books were burnt, including three quarters of all scientific libraries. The Nazis banned all but the most elementary education for Poles.

From the start, following the German invasion of Western Poland on 1 September 1939, and the Russian advance into Eastern Poland two weeks later, there was armed Polish resistance. The main force was eventually known as the Home Army (Armia Krajowa, or AK), and loyal to the Polish government in exile in London. The London government was based on the Peasant Party, Socialist Party and nationalists, excluding the Stalinists. The Home Army eventually organised over 200,000 fighters and existed alongside an underground state which provided schooling and courts.

As the Soviets drove the Nazis out, from 1944, they set up their own puppet government, the Polish Committee of National Liberation (PKWN). The Home

Army organised anti-German risings in advance of the Red Army, contending for power, aiming to take control before the Soviets arrived. However Home Army units were forcibly disbanded by the Russians and their fighters were either integrated into the Red Army or arrested or killed. The most important Home Army action was the Warsaw rising of August and September 1944. Stalin stopped the Soviet armies on the East Bank of the Vistula allowing the Nazis to smash the insurgency. Over 150,000 civilians were killed.

Poland had had a vigorous, mostly underground, workers' movement in the decades before World War I, and some years of a legal workers' movement in a more-or-less functioning bourgeois democracy in the early 1920s.

Stalin had disbanded the Polish Communist Party (KPP) in 1938, having murdered most of the leadership. According to Anne Applebaum, in *Gulag*, one estimate suggests 5,000 Polish Communists were murdered in the USSR between spring and summer of 1937. The Great Terror specifically singled-out Poles and launched the "Polish line of investigation" which led to the arrests of over 140,000 people during this phase of the Soviet purges. The NKVD had been told by Stalin to "beat the Poles for all you are worth."

Moscow-trained Stalinists were sent into Nazi-occupied Poland in 1942 but were either killed or arrested. Władysław Gomułka, who had avoided Stalin's purges of the late 30s because he was in a Polish jail, became the main leader of the underground Stalinist movement and then the key figure in the first phase of Stalinist government in Poland, from 1945-8. Around his leadership were gathered a distinct group of Polish Stalinists who had spent the War underground, in Poland. A second, ultra Moscow-loyal, grouping existed led by Bolesław Bierut.

The Gomułka wing was no less Stalinist than Bierut, but less servile to Stalin, more conscious of the need to take into account the hostility in Poland to the USSR and Russia's aggressive and imperialist relationship to Poland. According to Anne Applebaum (in *Iron Curtain*) Gomułka was said to have seen Stalin shouting at Bierut: 'What kind of fucking Communists are you?' in October 1944, when Bierut had suggested an all-out assault on the non-Communist-Party partisans might not be advisable. (The word "Communist", like the word "soviet", had lost its original meaning, and in everyday use now meant "Stalinist".)

The Home Army officially disbanded in January 1945. Shortly after sixteen former AK leaders were abducted and flown to Moscow where they were put on trial and jailed. Some Home Army fragments continued partisan warfare against the new Stalinist rulers. An amnesty in 1945 led to a decrease in AK numbers and activity. After then, most of the armed opposition was crushed, quickly; but some small groups continued fighting until the early 1950s.

A new Stalinist party, the Polish Workers' Party (PPR), was founded in

4

Władysław Gomułka (1905-82), the Polish Stalinist leader who ran the post-War Stalinist state until he was replaced by Bierut in 1948. Gomułka was again in power from 1956 until 1970. Gomułka cynically used antisemitism during the Stalinists' "anti-Zionist" campaign of 1967-8

January 1942 as a mechanism for Soviet policy in Poland. The PPR avoided using the word 'Communist' and presented itself as a patriotic anti-Nazi front. It said it was for democracy, land reform and nationalisation. PPR membership in July 1944 was 20,000. Membership went up to some hundreds of thousands in early 1945 and then down to 65,000 by the end of 1945, the result of purges and the revival of Stanisław Mikołajczyk's Peasant Party. In 1946 the Peasant Party had 600,000 members to the PPR's 235,000.

The PPR existed until 1948 when it merged with a heavily-purged wing of the Polish Socialist Party to create the Polish United Workers' Party (PZPR). In 1948 this Stalinist party had about a million members.

Stalinist Rule

At Yalta in February 1945 the Allies agreed that Poland should have a coalition government followed by free elections.

A land reform decree was issued in September 1944, benefiting a million smaller peasant families. 10,000 estates were taken, mainly from the rich and German owners, affecting about a fifth of the land. Land reform was one thing, but the peasants were wary of being forced into collective farms. Władysław Gomułka had studied at Stalin's Lenin School, in Moscow, in 1934-5, and had left with a very critical view of Soviet forced collectivisation. Gomułka told the Polish people he was against violent, forced collectivisation.

All factories employing more than 50 workers per shift were nationalised.

A broader provisional government was negotiated in 1945 with non-Communist forces fronting up a Stalinist state structure. This government was in place until the elections of 1947. The elections of 1947, and a referendum which preceded the election, were rigged and accompanied by great intimidation and violence. A million voters were disenfranchised and thousands of Peasant Party activists and 142 candidates were arrested.

Neal Ascherson describes the post-war period, prior to the "Stalinist onslaught [after 1948]" as a "moderate, open and responsive form of socialism [and was] thoroughly successful" (*The Polish August*). But the system he describes was neither moderate, open, responsive nor socialist. Yes, towns were rebuilt and industrial production increased as did the urban populations. But Poland was again occupied and oppressed. The new ruling power was a totalitarian state that had signed a pact with Hitler which destroyed Polish independence, was responsible for the mass murder at Katyn, and had allowed the 1944 Warsaw rising to fail and Warsaw to be destroyed.

State power was held by a Soviet force and its Polish agents who were in the process of systematically squeezing the political opposition to death, not just in Poland, but across Eastern Europe.

The Stalinist transformation of Eastern Europe was not unplanned by Stalin. It was not just a response to American power, as Ascherson seems to suggest (following Isaac Deutscher). It was a Stalinist policy which was necessary to retain political power. In big part the Cold War was the product of Soviet behaviour in Eastern Europe after 1945. Russian pressure forced Poland to renounce Marshall Plan money (instead Poland joined the Soviet economic bloc, Comecon, in 1949).

Half a million Soviet troops remained in Poland (and continued to do so, without legal basis, until 1956). The Soviet forces, including the NKVD, rounded up 150,000 Poles in the years 1945-8, executing many former Home Army members.

The new Soviet 'international', the Cominform, was founded in 1947. At its first conference Gomułka voted against the collectivisation of agriculture, defying the Russians.

Gomułka was suspected of insufficient loyalty to Moscow and the Soviets prepared his downfall. Gomułka petitioned Stalin, denouncing the Polish party as unpopular because it had too many prominent Jewish members. He argued it was necessary "to stop any further growth in the percentage of Jews in the state as well as the Party apparatus, but also to slowly lower that percentage, especially at the highest levels". He described Jewish Communists has having a 'national nihilism' – in other words, being insufficiently Polish.

On 3 September 1948 Bierut took Gomułka's place and Poland began its period of High Stalinism, which lasted until it "thawed" following Stalin's death in 1953.

In December 1948 Gomułka was removed from the Politburo. In November 1949 he was expelled from the Party. He was arrested in July 1951. Gomułka was released in 1954 and only rehabilitated in 1956. The Stalinist repression was less harsh in Poland than elsewhere in Eastern Europe. Gomułka escaped the period without a show trial and with his life.

In Hungary Rajk was accused of "Titoism" then executed. In Czechoslovakia Slánský and others faced an antisemitic campaign and were accused of "Trotskyite-Titoite-Zionism" and bourgeois nationalism. Slánský and ten others were hanged and their ashes mixed with dirt on a road outside Prague.

Timothy Garton Ash explains the uniqueness of Poland's experience of the worst phase of Stalinism in Eastern Europe in the following way in *The Polish Revolution*: the Polish communists were aware they were a beleaguered minority imposed by a hated foreign power "and simply could not afford to deplete their own ranks. Outside the Party, Stalinism was both too severe and too mild. It was too severe for the Party to win the voluntary cooperation of groups it just might have won by more conciliatory methods... it was too mild to break the back of civil society, as was done, for example in the three years of terror following the Russian invasion of Hungary in 1956.

"Even in the worst years of Stalinism Polish communism was distinguished by half-measures, partially executed. The Polish communists failed to collectivise private agriculture and to subjugate the Church." By 1956, the Poles had "retained an exceptional degree of independence in intellectual and cultural life."

Nevertheless, Poland was heavily oppressed. Up until 1956 Soviet officials were embedded in the Polish police, army and other state structures. A Soviet General, Konstantin Rokossovsky, was the government's Defence Minister after 1949.

By 1954 there were 84,200 political prisoners, with 6 million people – or one in three adults – on a secret police list of 'criminal and suspicious elements'. In 1953 there were 32,000 UB (Urząd Bezpieczeństwa, secret police) agents in Poland.

Bierut died in Moscow, in March 1956, shortly after attending the 20th Congress of the Communist Party at which Khrushchev denounced Stalin's crimes.

1956, Poznań

Stalin had died in March 1953. At the 20th Congress of the Soviet Communist Party in February 1956 Furst Secretary Nikita Khrushchev made his "Secret Speech" denouncing Stalin and the purges of the 1930s.

Bolesław Bierut, the "Polish Stalin" died in Moscow on 12 March 1956, shortly after attending the 20th Congress. Khrushchev went to Warsaw for the funeral, attempting to intervene in the discussions about who would replace Bierut. Apparently Khrushchev tried to have an orthodox Moscow-loyal Stalinist take over the Party; he also told the leadership there were too many Jews in leading positions. Edward Ochab, a reformer, got the job and many remaining political prisoners were released.

The Polish leadership allowed hundreds of meetings to take place in March and April 1956 to discuss Khrushchev's speech. The discussion spilled into dangerous areas that began to alarm the Communist establishment, who always had close concern for the Russian reaction to Polish events. Subjects being discussed included the Soviet massacre of Polish officers at Katyn in 1940, Stalin's refusal to help the Warsaw rising of August-September 1944 and the continued presence of Soviet forces on Polish soil.

In the Soviet Party Khrushchev was fighting Stalin loyalists. The political effects of his speech included winding down the gulag prison camp system, loosening the mechanisms of repression to some degree, and licencing a period of discussion and limited criticism of the Stalinist past. In Poland discussion raged, and included demands for a more independent, Polish, Communism.

Working-class anger had been growing during 1955. The Party's propaganda celebrated increased living standards and the successful completion of the Six Year plan. The workers knew the truth, however. Living standards had fallen by 30-40% between 1949 and 1955.

Poznań is a large industrial centre 300km west of Warsaw. At the biggest plant, the Joseph Stalin (Cegielski) metal works, a large delegation of workers was sent to see central government officials in the third week of June 1956.

The workers' complaints stemmed from the decisions made at a Party-sponsored economic conference in July 1953 which had raised industrial production norms and reduced take-home pay. The delegation demanded higher wages and a reduction in the norms. They returned on 26 June with promises which were then immediately cancelled.

11

Workers gather in the centre of Poznań, June 1956

At 6am on 28 June protests began. A big majority of the 15,000 Cegielski workers marched out in protest at losing their June bonus as a result of the rise in work quotas. The march grew as it descended on the town; by 10am over 100,000 workers were demonstrating in the city centre, demanding pay increases and reductions in prices. The protest turned into a riot when workers were led to believe their leaders had been arrested, probably provoked by state provocateurs. A prison was stormed, hundreds of prisoners released and arms looted. Communist offices, the courthouse and police stations were attacked and overrun. The first panicked shots were fired at the workers from government office windows, and tanks and armoured vehicles began to move into place around buildings still under state control.

The workers did not, in 1956, define themselves as root-and-branch against "Communism" as they understood it (Stalinism). Their demands were economic and when they spilled over into politics they were anti-Russian. The protesters sang the Internationale and demanded, "Russians go home!" Discontent was still often channelled through official Party organisation and the most prominent

Tanks under Russian control crush the movement in Poznań, late June 1956

workers' leader to emerge from the wave of protest was a young car worker, Leszek Gozdzik, secretary of his Party cell in his car plant (Timothy Garton Ash).

The rioting was eventually repressed by 10,000 troops and 400 tanks under the leadership of the Soviet general Rokossovsky who was in charge of all the armed forces in Poland. The Soviet state was determined to end the protests before they spread, as they had in East Germany in 1953.

The order to fire came from a Soviet officer. The chief of the Polish General Staff was a Soviet citizen, as were 76 other senior officers of the nominally Polish armed forces.

At least 75 people were killed, including a 13 year-old boy and five soldiers; 900 were badly injured. According to official statements 746 were arrested.

But why did Poznań erupt rather than any other Polish town? Why did the Cegielski Engineering workers lead the way? The first independent union organisation in Stalinist Poland was formed in the Cegielski works. In June 1956 the leaders in Section W-3 began attempting to bring together the various shops and sections in the plant in unified action, as well as linking up with workers at the Railway Repair Yards and other factories in the city. The worker-leaders planned various protest actions including silent demonstrations inside the factories, solidarity strikes and a march through the city during Poznań's International Trade

Fair. The independent worker activists in the Cegielski plant were the catalyst for the movement of 28 June but their protest became so massive, so rapidly, and their structure was so weak, that they lost the leadership of the movement in the face of the extreme state violence.

An absolutely central lesson for us from the Polish working-class protests in the decades leading up to the creation of Solidarność in 1980 is the key role played by worker activists (and worker-linked intellectuals) preparing struggles in advance — tenaciously, even through the worst of times, often after multiple arrests and persecution — and bringing lessons from previous battles into the present.

The Party in turmoil

On 29 June the Prime Minister, Józef Cyrankiewicz, declared on the local radio, "Any provocateur or lunatic who raises his hand against the people's government may be sure that this hand will be chopped off". Of the hundreds rounded up in Poznań many were tortured. However wages were also increased by as much as 50%. The Party began to haemorrhage members.

Inside the PZPR a faction began to agitate for the removal of the Soviet officers and for Polish control of Polish state forces. An emergency Central Committee was held in July and a set of reforms were agreed: limited liberalisation, more managerial freedom and a reduction in the size of the Party's bureaucracy. The reformers demanded that Władysław Gomułka be returned to power. Fearing the workers and their withering authority the Central Committee readmitted Gomułka to the Party in August. Gomułka demanded the role of First Party Secretary and the sacking of his Moscow-line enemies in the leadership.

The reformers began to spread their fight into the factories, encouraging the formation of workers' councils. In September a council was formed at the Żerań car factory north of Warsaw. The councils quickly spread across the country, manipulated by reform Communists against old-style Stalinists.

The man taking the leading role was Władysław Gomułka.

On 19 October, unannounced, Khrushchev flew into Warsaw with most of the leadership of the Russian Party. Simultaneously he ordered the mobilisation of Soviet troops in Poland and told them to march on Warsaw. Gomułka declared he was perfectly capable of taking care of Poland and ordered Interior Ministry troops loyal to him to take positions in defence of Warsaw. General Wacław Komar — who had been tortured and imprisoned in the Stalinist period — blocked a Soviet armoured column as it approached Warsaw. The Polish Party called on the workers to be prepared to resist.

On 20 October the PZPR leadership brought Gomułka back into the Politburo and elected him First Secretary.

Khrushchev backed down, saying, "Finding a reason for armed conflict now would be very easy. But finding a way to put an end to such a conflict later on would be very hard." Rokossovsky was removed and in return Gomułka promised to follow Soviet foreign policy and remain in the Warsaw Pact.

Khrushchev might have demanded more, except for the fact that the Polish events were feeding into discontent in Hungary, which would quickly lead to the

Hungarian workers' revolution, and the Russian invasion of October/November 1956. A Hungarian student protest march in Budapest, in support of Gomułka, was one of the events in the immediate lead-up to the Hungarian rising.

The events in Hungary — enormous violence following the invasion, and vast repression against the workers' revolution — then haunted all those who demanded Polish reform. In hundreds of meetings across Poland in the final months of 1956 – hosted by the PZPR or the state-run unions — Poles demanded an end to Russian domination. The fact that the movement in Poland did not go further was partly due to the terror in Hungary. Gomułka encouraged a purge of old-style Stalinists at local level. But he also warned against going further – a movement like Hungary risked a general rising across Eastern Europe and the possibility of major war. Nevertheless Soviet symbols and buildings were attacked in November.

The Party regained some credibility, mainly because it had stood up for Poland against the Soviet Union. Gomułka rode the nationalist wave and loyalty to him was essentially nationalist. For a period Gomułka was immensely popular; a massive demonstration in Warsaw, on 24 October — as Soviet troops entered Hungary to crush the workers' rising — expressed support for Gomułka.

In mid-November Gomułka went to Russia and concluded a deal which ended the direct supervision by Soviet officials of the Polish executive. Poles imprisoned in the USSR were released and could return home. The integration of the Polish economy as a subset of the Soviet economy was replaced by a more equitable trading relationship. And the status of Soviet troops in Polish territory was normalised by a treaty.

Reforms were rolled out in Poland. For the moment the press was relatively free of censorship. Western books and films were permitted and the state stopped blocking western radio stations. The Catholic Church was able to choose its own leadership and Gomułka even allowed it to begin teaching Catholic theology in state schools. The Primate, Cardinal Wyszyński, returned to Warsaw after three years internment in a remote monastery.

Secret police numbers were cut and the UB, now renamed Security Service (SB), was brought under the control of the Interior Ministry, and so under Party control. Terror ceased to be the central instrument of rule and the leading role of the Party meant the elite's security was guaranteed. By the end of the 1950s PZPR membership stood at about a million, the lowest since its foundation in 1948. Many of those that were left were Party officials or those that directly benefited from one-party rule. Only 30% of Party officials had any secondary education. Many had been deliberately recruited from plebeian layers of society in an effort to give the regime stability.

By 1956 a little less than 10% of Polish agriculture had been collectivised. During the 'Polish October' 80% of agricultural collectives were broken up. The peasants did not wait for legislation but began to abolish the collectives and resumed cultivation as small proprietors. By 1960 small farms (0.5-5 hectares) represented 53% of the total and "dwarf farms" (under 3 hectares) over 40%.

Gomułka's popularity withered, slowly. By 1957 working-class living standards were some of the lowest in Europe, and the economy stagnated. The workers' councils which had taken on some real life and fought for — and had won — wage increases gradually had their autonomy choked off by the state. In early 1957 the conference of workers' councils was denounced as an "anarchist utopia." Later that year a strike of tram workers in Łódź was crushed, in October demonstrations in Warsaw were dispersed; an opposition journal was closed and the monolithic structure of the Party was restored.

Open Letter to the Party

The first years after 1956 were years of disillusion and slow-down. Much of the intellectual discontent came from those advocating a "liberal-Communist" turn from the authorities.

On 14 November 1964 Jacek Kuroń and Karol Modzelewski, young lecturers at the University of Warsaw, had a document confiscated by the police during a raid on their apartment. The police had taken the first draft and only copy of what would become "An Open Letter to the Party". On 27 November they were both expelled from the Party.

Their 95-page Open Letter was written to explain their views. It opens in this way, describing the ruling class: "According to official doctrine, we live in a socialist country. This thesis is based on the identification of state ownership of the means of production with social ownership... State ownership of the means of production... is exercised by those social groups to which the state belongs... To whom does power belong in our state? To one monopolistic Party — the Polish United Workers' Party (PZPR)... The Party is not only monopolistic, but is also organized along monolithic lines... The bureaucracy exercises the totality of political and economic power, depriving the working class not only of the means of power and control, but even of self-defence...

"It is said that the bureaucracy cannot be a class, since the individual earnings of its members do not come anywhere near the individual earnings of capitalists; since no bureaucrat, taken by himself, rules anything more than his mansion, his car, and his secretary; since entrance to the bureaucratic ranks is determined by a political career and not by inheritance; and since it is relatively easy to be eliminated from the bureaucracy in a political showdown. This is quite wrong. All the above arguments prove only the obvious: the property of the bureaucracy is not of an individual nature, but constitutes the collective property of an elite which identifies itself with the state."

The authors describe in great detail the immiseration and exploitation of the working class:

"In 1962, the productive worker in industry created, on the average, a product worth 7,100 złoty, out of which he received, as a working wage, a monthly average of 2,200 złoty. In other words, for one-third of the working day, the worker creates a subsistence minimum for himself, and for the remaining two-thirds, the surplus product.

Jacek Kuroń (1934-2004), left, and Karol Modzelewski (1937-2019), right.

Kuroń and Modzelewski co-wrote the Open Letter to the Party (1964) for which they were expelled and jailed. Kuroń become a key theoretician of the underground opposition of the 1970s and advocate of the 'self-limiting revolution'

"The working class has no influence on the size of the surplus product, on its use and distribution, since… it is deprived of influence on the decisions of the authorities, who have at their disposal the means of production and the labour product itself. It is not the working class that fixes the working wage — that wage is imposed from above, just as are the production norms (at one and the same time). The workers have no rights of, and no way of engaging in, economic self-defence, since they are deprived of any organization of their own, and any effective strike action must be organised. Any organisation of workers aimed at carrying on a struggle for higher wages is illegal and, as such, prosecuted by the power apparatus — the police, attorney general's office, and the courts."

The document describes underproduction, waste, poor quality of finished goods, and low technical levels in the Stalinist economy.

The bureaucratic, dysfunctional system encouraged lying and manipulation of data. "The worker tries to lower efficiency and hides the reserves in his sector to delay the change in norms; he makes a product of inferior quality in order to meet the norm more easily. The manager will ignore the poor product because of the 'factory's interest,' i.e., production of quantity instead of quality. The management hides reserves in order to obtain lower plan figures, chooses [methods] to carry out the plan more easily, tries to escape production of labour-consuming

19

Ludwik Hass (1918-2008) was a Polish Trotskyist. This photograph was taken after his arrest. Russia 1939

export goods and to avoid technological progress, improvement or modernization achieved at the expense of the enterprise."

Kuroń and Modzelewski concluded that a workers' revolution was necessary to overturn the rule of the Stalinist, bureaucratic ruling class. Their programme:

• Workers' control of factories.

• Legislative and executive power to be in the hands of a federation of workers' councils.

• Multi-party system, freedom of speech and organisations, no censorship.

• Free, independent trade unions.

• The political activisation of the working class. Providing necessary education of workers for that purpose.

• Abolition of political police and of the regular army. The functions of the army to be taken over by workers' militia.

• In agriculture both collectivisation and free market to be avoided. Problems to be solved by the establishment of an autonomous political representation of peasant producers.

• International solidarity of the working class.

The authors had a clear blueprint for a future workers' state. It is less clear that they knew how to achieve their aims, in particular how to destroy the existing state and counter the threat of Soviet invasion. The Open Letter discusses the peaceful development of an anti-bureaucratic revolution, rather than the inevitability of violent confrontation. The least convincing section deals with the possibility of Soviet invasion against an anti-bureaucratic workers' revolution. The document does not clearly state Poland is oppressed by "Soviet" (Russian) imperialism nor that Poland has the right to self determination, making the true but very general point, "Our ally against the intervention of Soviet tanks is the Russian, Ukrainian, Hungarian and Czech working class."

The key to facing down, or defeating Soviet imperialism lay in the willingness to fight for Polish self-determination. In recent history, in 1956, the defeated workers' rising in Hungary provided part of the answer (in negative form), that the workers must arm themselves and fight; and Gomułka's willingness to mobilise Polish troops against Khrushchev in 1956 formed another element of a solution. A Polish workers' revolution must win over, or neutralise, or defeat, Polish state forces and turn some of them round to defend the nation and the revolution.

Perhaps the authors felt unable to write all they would have wanted to write.

Later, in July 1965, Kuroń was sentenced to three years and Modzelewski three and a half years in prison for publishing their Open Letter. Kuroń sang the Internationale in the dock.

Ludwik Hass, the veteran Polish Trotskyist, who had been arrested by the Soviets in 1939 and had only been released from the notorious gulag at Vorkuta in 1956, edited the Open Letter. Hass was sentenced to three years. Kazimierz Badowski — also a Trotskyist — and the former Trotskyist Romuald Śmiech were also jailed.

Isaac Deutscher, Trotsky's biographer and a member of the pre-war Polish Trotskyist group in Poland, wrote a letter to Gomułka protesting about the persecution of his socialist opponents, secret trials, and long sentences. Deutscher contrasted the selflessness of the defendants — who had raised their chained fists and sung the Internationale in court — with the sycophancy of Gomułka's own supporters. Deutscher wrote: "May I remind you of your own words [of] October 1956? 'The cult of the personality was not a matter just of Stalin's person', you stated then. 'This was a system which had been transplanted from the USSR to nearly all Communist Parties... *We have finished, or rather we are finishing, with that system once and for all.*' But are you not to some extent re-establishing that system? Do you wish these trials to mark the tenth anniversary of your own rehabilitation and of that 'Spring in October', during which you raised so many hopes for the future?"

Hass was arrested by the Russian Stalinists and sent to the Vorkuta gulag; on his return to Poland in 1957 he declared that he remained a revolutionary socialist who wanted the overthrow of the Polish bureaucracy. Here Hass, (centre left) is addressing an academic conference, 1981.

• Ludwik Hass was born into a middle-class Polish-Jewish family in 1918. He became a Trotskyist at Lvov University. When the Second World War started he found himself in the Soviet-occupied area. The Trotskyists produced a journal in Nazi-occupied Poland for three years until most of their comrades were murdered; in the Soviet area the Trotskyists found it even harder, and the NKVD immediately arrested Hass who was deported to the gulag and apparently escaped execution by bureaucratic muddle. In the camps he was given office work, rather than work down a mine — which saved his life. He was among the last to be repatriated, in 1957. On his arrival at Warsaw station he announced to those that met him that his intention was the overthrow of the bureaucracy; he sang the Internationale and raised his fist. Hass died in 2008, remaining a Trotskyist.

• Kazimierz Badowski had become a Polish Communist Party member in 1924 or 25, while still at school. He was jailed in 1926 for "anti-state activity" and became a Trotskyist while studying in Belgium. He joined the Polish Trotskyist group, the Union of Communist Internationalists, in 1933 and worked as a chemist in Poland under Nazi occupation. He was jailed by the Stalinists for four years in 1946. At the age of nearly 60, in the courtroom in December 1965 and January 1966, he – alongside Hass — turned the trial into a political demonstration, openly making the case for Trotsky and revolutionary socialism. He remained a Trotskyist until his death in 1990.

1968: antisemitism

"There are certain situations in which any honest person should consider himself Jewish" – Jacek Kuroń

The student protests and repression of March 1968 and the anti-Jewish agitation and purge of 1967-8 have several roots.

Following Gomułka's triumph of 1956 groupings formed in the ruling Party — a pro-Soviet faction (the Natolin group) and a 'reformist' group who were opposed to High Stalinism in the name of a less repressive authoritarianism (Puławianie). Both groups were named after the area of Warsaw where the tendency met. Natolin's members were authoritarian, anti-intellectual and antisemitic. Puławianie, the 'revisionists', included Jewish Stalinists. Natolin nicknamed Puławianie as 'Yids'.

Natolin's supporters called for a purge of Jews from leading Party positions blaming them alone for the crimes committed in Poland during Stalin's rule.

Natolin was at first defeated, then, after Gomułka abandoned reforming the system he turned towards them considering reform Communism a bigger danger.

In the period 1956-8 a further 40,000 Jews left Poland, leaving only 30,000 by 1960.

In the early '60s a section in the Ministry of Internal Affairs built an index of all Jewish members of the PZPR. Military counterintelligence created a similar index of Jewish army personnel.

By the late '50s Natolin and Puławianie had faded. Some of Natolin's ideas, however, were continued by an alliance known as the Partisans. The Partisans retained Natolin's antisemitism and anti-intellectualism but replaced Natolin's willingness to subordinate to Poland to the USSR with Polish nationalism. Their leader was Mieczysław Moczar. Many of the group's central supporters had been part of the Communist underground in Nazi-occupied Poland. Stalin had considered this group unreliable, and had purged them in the late 40s. After Gomułka's victory in 1956 many had come back into the state apparatus and by the early 1960s they had become a serious force, looking for overdue promotions and power.

Moczar became leader of a movement, the Union of Fighters for Freedom and Democracy, which included former Home Army members as well as Stalinists. By 1962 it had, perhaps, a quarter of a million members.

The antisemitic campaign was launched by Gomułka in a speech of 19 July

23

1967 to the official, state-run, fake trade union conference, following the Israeli victory against the Arab states in the Six Day War of June 1967. The Israeli victory was a disaster for Moscow's foreign policy and Moscow had broken off diplomatic relations with Israel on 10 June 1967, closely followed by other Eastern European states.

Referring to the Israeli victory Gomułka denounced the "Zionists" who supported "the Israeli aggressor and imperialism" and who were forming a "Fifth column" inside the country which endangered Poland. "Fifth column" had been used extensively in underground publications during the war, referring to Nazi-collaborators. Placards carried by workers on demonstrations, and displayed at Party meetings declared, "Down with the 'New Fifth Column'".

Rallies against "Israeli imperialism" were held in towns and workplaces. The campaign was then enthusiastically taken up by Moczar, the Minister of Internal Affairs since 1964, and the Partisan faction through the major Party papers and the security apparatus.

In the press and the Party intellectual dissent and the desire for freedom of expression became synonymous with support for Israel. All Jews became "Zionists" and revisionist intellectuals "Zionist sympathisers", as Gomułka used the campaign against the 'liberal' reform wing in the Party and to shore up his position against Moczar. The main theme was that the Zionists/Jews were ungrateful and duplicitous guests who were acting as agents for Israel, America and West Germany while living amongst the Polish people. 150 Jews were purged from the armed forces and Leon Kasman, editor of *Trybuna Ludu*, the leading Party newspaper was sacked.

All Zionist political and cultural organisations had been banned in 1949-50. Any remaining Jews who had been supporters of Zionism had left in the '40s and 50s. The hunt for "Zionists" was taking place in a country without Zionists and where the remaining Jews were a very tiny minority.

Now the funding of Polish Jewish cultural organisations by American Jewish institutions was prohibited, and many of these Jewish groups ceased functioning. A poem by the poet, Antoni Słonimski, which praised Israel's struggle, was banned from publication.

The government-sponsored antisemitic campaign found a hearing in the broader population. Franciszek Całka, a Jew who was head of the Predom factory in Warsaw, reported that the local PZPR branch in the suburb of Żoliborz favoured dismissing all Jews from the factory. The Chair of the branch also stated, "Poland should be run by Poles, and Jews are not Poles."

The daughter of Zenon Kliszko, a close ally of Gomułka, was forced to break off her engagement to her Jewish fiancé and forbidden to have contact with

A state-organised May Day demonstration, 1968. The placards read:
"Down with Zionists' provocations!"
"Vietnamese people: we support you"
"Down with Zionism: agency of imperialism"
"Socialism is future of mankind"

people of Jewish origin. The campaign was conducted despite Gomułka's wife Zofia being Jewish (born Liwa Szoken, into an Orthodox family).

Józef Lidwon, in a letter of May 1968 to the weekly *Polityka*, and asking the editors to condemn antisemitism, wrote: "For some time my daughter has been coming back from school crying because the children do not want to play with her because they think she is a Jewess. In fact she is not Jewish, but it is below human dignity to explain such a thing to everybody." *Polityka*, edited by Mieczysław Rakowski, who much later would later become First Secretary of the Party, was the only major paper that refused to publish anti-Jewish propaganda (Joanna Beate Michlic, *Poland's Threatening Other*).

In Czechoslovakia, where there was a similar persecution of Jews along with the widespread destruction of synagogues, 300 writers wrote in support of artistic freedom and against antisemitism.

On 12 December 1968, Bertrand Russell addressed an open letter to Polish Prime Minister Władysław Gomułka in which he wrote: "By some twisted logic, all Jews are now Zionists, Zionists are fascists, fascists are Nazis, and Jews, therefore, are to be identified with the very criminals who only recently sought to eliminate Polish Jewry."

From late April 1968 Gomułka decided the antisemitic campaign had outlived its usefulness – it was creating a degree of internal criticism and conflict inside the Party and state — and he began to rein it in. It took months to do so. Decisively, in July, Gomułka removed Mieczysław Moczar from head of the Ministry of Internal Affairs, removing him from his power base. The Central Committee Plenum of 8-9 July officially ended the "anti-Zionist" campaign although obstruction from sections of the SB secret police, military and others, continued.

1968: the student protests

Kuroń and Modzelewski's jailing was part of the conflict of reform Communism with the Party-state machine. This phase of history was finally ended during the late 60s and led to future opposition movements being constituted outside the Party, in opposition to it.

University and intellectual life had become an area of contested space. 1968 was the point when the reformist 'liberal Stalinist' current came into direct conflict with the mainstream Party and the state.

The 1968 events in Poland took place alongside the general strike and student revolt in France and, nearer to home, the vast political crisis which developed in Czechoslovakia during the spring and summer. In January 1968 a Slovak Stalinist, Alexander Dubček, became First Secretary of the Czechoslovakian Communist Party. As in Poland, the Czechoslovak economy was performing poorly. In order to reform a sclerotic system Dubček initiated a series of reforms which led to greater freedoms. Dubček became enormously popular but, simultaneously, mobilised the local Stalinists against his reforms and greatly alarmed the Russians. On 20-21 August Warsaw Pact armies – including the Polish — invaded Czechoslovakia and put and end to the 'Prague Spring'.

The unfortunate lasting lesson the Polish opposition took from Czechoslovakia 1968 (and the extraordinarily violent invasion of Hungary in 1956) was that no matter how powerful an opposition movement was inside an Eastern Bloc state, its ability to make political reforms was limited by the threat of a Russian invasion. However, in the first half of 1968, the Polish students were encouraged by the movement Dubček had unleashed.

The Polish student protests of March 1968 began with the banning of a production of a play by the nineteenth century poet Adam Mickiewicz. *Dziady* (Forefathers' Eve), written in 1824, depicted the Polish struggle for freedom against Russian despotism. It contains lines such as these:

"Am I to be free? Yes! Where this news came from I do not know, but I am alive to what it means to be free under the hands of a Muscovite. These scoundrels? They only take the fetters off my hands and feet, but crush my soul." And: "Moscow only sends rogues to Poland."

These lines brought audiences to their feet, cheering and clapping. So the Polish censors acted to ban the play. At the end of the last performance on 30 January 1968 the audience applauded for half an hour and then marched into

27

Warsaw, where the students were attacked by the police.

The play's director, Kazimierz Dejmek, was expelled from the Party and then sacked from the National Theatre.

At the beginning of March 1968 Adam Michnik and Henryk Szlajfer — Jewish students — were both expelled from Warsaw University for their part in dissident activities. On 8 March several thousand students marched in protest, in their defence.

Jacek Kuroń, released in 1967, was arrested again. Protests spread to all the major university towns across Poland. Politically the students still looked towards reforming Polish "Socialism", calling for liberal reforms, but stressing their loyalty. They wanted academic freedom, an end to censorship and decentralisation in the economy. They stressed the bond between the workers and the intellectuals, but were isolated and failed to win support in the working class.

The philosopher Leszek Kołakowski summed up the reform Communists' attitudes: "Let us consider the appalling and miserable system of information in the press, let us consider the restrictions and harassment practiced in Poland in the humanities, in current history, sociology, political science and law. Let us consider the poor, deplorable discussions in which no one ever says what is really the matter, for everything leads to forbidden fruit... I imagine a kind of socialist life in which this unbearable and destructive state of affairs... shall be abolished. We want the abolition of such a situation in the name of socialism, not against it."

It would take another eight years for an intellectual opposition to re-emerge. And when it did it would flatly oppose the regime.

Kuroń told the court, "The examining officers made a great effort to find a Jewish name amongst my ancestors. When they were not able, however, to make a Jew of me, they tried to make me at least a Ukrainian. There were days during the pre-trial proceedings that I was ready to become a Jew. For there are certain situations in which any honest person should consider himself Jewish."

Kuroń and Modzelewski received three-and-a-half years in January 1969. A month later Adam Michnik got three years. From the dock Michnik said, "[I want] more freedom, more justice, more equality. [I want] the windows of our houses to look towards the sun."

At least 13,000 Poles of Jewish origin emigrated in 1968–72 as a result of being fired from their positions and various other forms of harassment. There were now under 10,000 Jews left in Poland.

The West German state was a particular problem for Gomułka in the 1960s as, until a change of government in 1969, the Federal Republic did not recognise Poland's western frontier, on the Oder-Neisse rivers. Gomułka was concerned the USSR would do a deal with the West Germans which would disadvantage Poland by altering the border in West Germany's favour. In 1970 West Germany signed agreements with the USSR and Poland recognising Poland's Western border and so abolishing one of the justifications for Poland's unequal relationship with the USSR, that Poland needed Russian help against the threat of a border dispute with Germany.

1970 on the Northern Coast

Gomułka, raised to power and popularity by his opposition to the Soviet state in 1956 was now only in power because of Soviet backing. He was seriously weakened and his rule would last only until the events of late 1970.

On Saturday 12 December 1970 Warsaw announced major price increases with immediate effect. Meat, already in short supply, became more expensive, rising in price by 17% two weeks before Christmas. The Party had raised prices in this way three times before: in 1953, 59 and 65. The theory was that if the price rises were staggered there would be panic buying, and hoarding, and a boost to the black market.

The opposition movement grew from Monday morning. Party offices were attacked by shipyard workers in the port of Gdańsk (formerly Danzig). Later in the week strikes and occupations spread across the northern port cities. Street fighting took place in Gdynia and Szczecin with dozens shot down, including 13 on their way to work in the Paris Commune yard in Gdynia. In the port of Szczecin (formerly the German city Stettin) in the far north west of Poland, workers' action was taking place in 120 workplaces; workers had formed a town-wide strike committee which ran supplies and kept order. The Szczecin workers demanded, for the first time, "independent trade unions under the authority of the working class."

Under pressure from the workers and from the Soviet leadership who were demanding a peaceful solution, Gomułka had a stroke. Gomułka was replaced by Edward Gierek, a Party boss from Upper Silesia. The Russians preferred Gierek to Moczar, the vociferous Polish nationalist.

Gierek went on television and apologised. He also promised wage increases for the lowest paid and a price freeze. That calmed the situation for a period, but the movement erupted again in January 1971.

By mid-January meetings in the coastal shipyards and factories were demanding justice for those killed in December and the release of those arrested, in addition to questions of wages and prices. The government had mobilised 61,000 soldiers and used 3,000 tanks and armoured cars against the workers' rebellion and at least forty workers had been killed and over a thousand wounded.

Strikes began to break out again in Gdańsk. On the afternoon of 24 January Gierek, and his new Prime Minister Piotr Jaroszewicz, turned up at the occupied Warski yard in Szczecin. They debated the strikers for nine hours and repeated

A jeep stands burning in a rock-littered street, Gdańsk, December 1970

their performance the next day in Gdańsk. Gierek begged for the workers' support, and eventually got it.

Gierek insisted, however, that the price rises of December had to remain. He backed down when the women textile workers of Łódź struck in mid-February and the old food prices were restored on 1 March 1971. Neal Ascherson commented, "December 1970 also confirmed the split in the Polish opposition... Intellectuals took almost no part in the events. In March 1968 the students of Gdańsk Polytechnic had announced 'We solidarise ourselves above all with the Polish working class,' but they received no support from that class. [In] December 1970 the shipyard workers marched to the Gdańsk Polytechnic and called on the students to join them. They stayed indoors."

The movement of December 1970-February 1971 was of workers alone; the movement of 1968 was students alone.

The aftermaths of the events of 1970

Q. What's the difference between Gomułka and Gierek?
A. There is no difference, only Gierek does not understand that yet.

The Party's Eighth Plenum assembled in February 1971. Gomułka was suspended from the Central Committee and his allies Kliszko and Jaszczuk were expelled. Moczar survived until later that year before being removed; his 'Partisan' faction then finally crumbled and disappeared.

Gierek, previously leader of the "technocrats" faction in the Party, now focussed on raising living standards as a route to social stability. In the early 1970s growth rates increased, as did real wages – by 40% in the first half of the 70s — and the production of consumer goods, including Fiat cars made under licence. The USSR gave hard currency credits so Poland could buy from the West, and the US gave credit to buy grain.

In 1972 National Income rose by 10%. In 1973 the rise was even higher. It became easier to travel abroad, to the West, and easier to get dollars.

Further market reforms freed up agriculture. Peasant taxes were cut and compulsory selling to the state was abolished. There were yet more attempts to decentralise industrial management; plants in the same industry were grouped together and managers were given power to vary wages and reward increased productivity.

Western industrial equipment imports averaged $100m per year under Gomułka; in the early 70s this figure multiplied rapidly. By 1974 it stood at $1.9bn; production was hit by the oil price hike after 1973.

Poland's foreign debt was $700m in 1970. By 1975 it stood at $6bn.

The easing of censorship in 1971 was reimposed, gradually. Shortages began to appear in shops as the state channelled good for export in an attempt to control the balance of trade. The Party further centralised control, reigned in the industrial decentralisation, and attacked the peasantry's right to inherit.

Gdańsk. Workers move on as fires burn in the background. During the street fighting of December 1970 thouands of troops and militarised police were used; Over 40 people were killed and 1,000 injured and the Stalinist state repressed the working-class movement.

In Szczecin, December 1970, local Party and state "union" offices were set on fire, and the police headquarters was attacked. Workers fought street battles with the police.

There was a local general strike. At the centre of events were the Warski Shipyard workers who occupied their yard and set up a workers' militia. The workers' strike committee included Party members. In January 1971 the workers negotiated concessions from Gierek.

The explosion, June 1976

The price of meat had been frozen in 1970 and the freeze remained intact until mid-1976. The state feared popular rebellion. On 24 June the Prime Minister, Piotr Jaroszewicz, announced meat price rises of around 70%. Sugar was to double in price, butter and cheese were to rise by 60%, poultry and vegetables were to go up by 30%, rice by 150%.

The state prepared for trouble by mobilising the army and militia. On the day before the announcement the army took to the streets of Gdańsk in a show of strength. Some political dissidents and known workers' leaders were conscripted, including Jacek Kuroń.

By now the workers had learnt that they had to power to stop such rises by going into the streets in large numbers. The next day masses of workers struck demanding the increases be rescinded. Strike committees were formed in many enterprises. The strike only lasted a single day before Jaroszewicz was back on television to concede defeat. The Party had suffered a serious blow and its authority was further eroded. Gierek would have liked to have got rid of Jaroszewicz, blaming him for the crisis; he was constrained because Jaroszewicz was close to the Russians.

At the tractor factory in Ursus, a working-class suburb of Warsaw, most of the workers had stopped work. The workers had struck in February 1971 in response to the last round of increases. At 9am a senior manager and the Party secretary at the plant, Stanisław Maćkowski, had been surrounded and a woman worker had slapped both of them.

Workers joined with people from the town to occupy the rail lines and prevented the Paris-Moscow express from moving. 1,000 demonstrators sat on the track.

The workers had not been troubled by the police during the day, and the protests had been peaceful. Later, after 8pm, after the workers had won and begun to disperse they were attacked by police and ZOMO paramilitary units who used great violence. The police riot lasted all night and many workers were beaten up and assaulted while in custody. It turned out that police spies had mixed among the crowds marking protesters with a solution visible under ultraviolet light which was used to identify some of the leaders.

The largest protests were in Radom, south east of Warsaw. The strikes began at the Walter Metal factory which produced small arms and ammunition. When

34

the workers attempted to arm themselves, they failed because the boss, factory director Skrzypek, had moved all the ammunition to a local air base. After 8:30am workers began to leave the factory to visit other local factories. Workers at a tin can factory, leather workers and workers from a heating factory joined in.

Marching with red and white flags and singing the Internationale and the Polish national anthem they marched down May First Street to the PZPR committee building. Chanting, "We want to eat!" they were joined by students, housewives, and workers from tobacco plants, rail repair, telephone and many smaller factories. By 9:40 there were 6,000 workers in front of the PZPR office. The Deputy Secretary Adamczyk came out and told them he could not discuss with a "rabble." A woman with a child stepped out of the crowd and told him she was a widow with three children and she could not afford to feed them. She asked him how much he made. Adamczyk told her if she was so concerned about her children she should have left them at home, at which point she took her shoe off and began to hit him on the head with it.

Adamczyk demanded they pick a committee so he could negotiate. A woman worker shouted, "Yes, so then you'll know who to arrest." A man stepped out from the crowd saying his work clothes were filthy but he could only afford one set of clothes per year, when he need four. He demanded to know how much Adamczyk's clothes cost. The crowd then started chanting, "Strip him!" A group of young workers did precisely that and Adamczyk fled back to the Party building in his underwear followed by a barrage of stones and rubble.

By mid-morning barricades were being built and the mood swung against the Party. Bonfires were built and many threw their Party cards on it. The red flag was removed from the building and the Polish national flag hoisted.

By midday the state was airlifting SB officers and army forces with special riot equipment into the area. When meat supplies were discovered inside the Party building, and then displayed to the crowd, demonstrators began to systematically destroy the Party's HQ. As the building burned ZOMO units and firefighters tried to get to the building. More barricades went up and the crowd, now estimated at 40,000, attacked with Molotov cocktails and stones. A meat factory was over-run and ham marked for export was looted.

24 vehicles were destroyed and 75 police injured during the fighting in Radom. An unknown number of workers were killed or injured, but in the aftermath 2,000 were arrested in the Radom area.

On the coast, in the Tri-city area of Gdańsk, Gdynia and Sopot, the workers in Gdynia began a sit-in strike early in the morning. Workers from Gdynia went to Gdańsk and blocked the entrance and as the shifts changed the Gdańsk workers also began to strike. The Regional Party Secretary, Tadeusz Fiszbach, together with the state union representative, went to meet the workers. Fiszbach began, "Comrades!" and was met by, "Comrades — that is you, the Bureaucracy, the Dictatorship's people." The workers demanded to know how much Fiszbach earned; others said they didn't want to have to work 300 hours a month, in 12 hour days, simply to feed their families.

The Gdańsk shipyard workers, aware of their strength, demanded that Gierek come and see them, immediately. They declared they would not leave the yard and by 1pm they – almost unanimously – had called for a general strike to start at 9am the following morning.

Strikes also took place in Płock, Grudziądz, at the repair shipyard in Szczecin, a power plant in Gryfino, a bearings factory in Poznań and in many other towns across the country. In Łódź, the textile centre which had been a strike centre in 1971, at least sixteen factories were hit by industrial action. But no workers went out into the streets – they were now wary of being shot down.

A speech made to a mass meeting by Zdzisław Bednarek, a workers' representative at the Transformer and Traction Apparatus factory in Łódź, was later reprinted. He said that the workers had promised to help Gierek in 1971 but had been let down; the consultations with the workers that had been promised had not happened; those responsible for the economic crisis should be held to account. He said that no-one wanted a repetition of the bloodshed of 1970 and that the workers did not want to return to capitalism, but they did want free trade unions and parliamentary democracy.

The strike had won, and the workers immediately returned to work, but now the State took its revenge. Strike centres were subjected to serious repression. The European TUC estimated that 20,000 people lost their jobs and 6,000 were arrested. The Party held a series of mass meetings in support of the government. In Gdańsk an official demonstration was held attended by managers and office workers and Party members, often bussed in from outside. When the march reached the main square bystanders laughed at them.

At the Ursus Tractor factory the Party's factory committee secretary gave a speech blaming the trouble on, "anarchists, brawlers, enemies of true working people, old malcontents, troublemakers, drunkards, provocateurs and hooligans." Over the next few months groups of Ursus workers received harsh prison sentences; perhaps as many as 1,750 workers were dismissed.

In Radom police round-ups went on for several weeks; activists suspect that police also murdered three people in the days after the riot. In July and August 26 workers were sentenced to between two and ten years jail. Within ten days a lesser court had tried 5,000 others who often faced fines or three months in jail.

Elsewhere there were mass sackings. At the Lenin shipyard in Gdańsk 200-400

36

On 25 June 1976 workers at the Ursus tractor factory struck and blocked rail lines in protest against food price rises.

were sacked; workers were dismissed at four factories in Warsaw; 300 were sacked at fourteen factories in Łódź. The situation was similar in other strike centres.

The themes of these strikes were: skilled workers took the lead; the demands were mainly economic and the strikes quickly subsided once the government caved in and removed the rises. Unlike 1970-1 when the strikes were mainly confined to the Baltic coast and Łódź, the movement of June 1976 was national. The workers were often reluctant to elect strike committees which would later mean the bosses had a list of people to arrest.

The state had also learned lessons from 1970. The state forces did not use firearms and the army was kept out of the fighting. ZOMO paramilitary police forces were used widely for the first time.

1976: the aftermath

KOR. The intellectuals link with the workers

In the wake of the events of June 1976 a massive expansion of opposition activity and organisation took place. Unique in the Eastern Bloc a large number of industrial workers took part.

The Church also protested. Wyszyński defended the victimised workers and demanded an amnesty in July 1976. Clubs of Catholic Intelligentsia (KIK) were active.

Activists who became the core of the Workers' Defence Committee (KOR, Komitet Obrony Robotników) began work to provide legal, medical and financial support from the first trial of Ursus workers, which began on 17 July 1976. They also began to publish open letters and manifestos in defence of the workers. The first was "The Declaration of the 14 in Solidarity with the Workers," which was published immediately after the June violence and was sent to the Sejm (Parliament). The Declaration of the 14 demanded free association, a free press and "real representation of the workers" since the official union organisation, the CRZZ, had shown its inability to do so. Money came initially from Warsaw intellectuals but the appeal quickly spread across the country and included priests making collections; two committees were set up abroad to raise funds. In the first year they gathered a large sum, the equivalent of $47,000.

Work in support of Radom workers began a little later, in September. The final impulse to found KOR followed the detention of support workers attending a trial in Radom. The worst treatment was dished out to a Jewish activist who was subjected to antisemitic abuse and knocked unconscious.

In September 1976 fourteen intellectuals, mainly from Warsaw, founded KOR. Their initial members were deliberately older and with some social prominence as a limited precaution against state repression. The majority of the committee had been politically active in the inter-war period; nine had been active in the non-communist resistance movement during World War 2, and five had been active in the Polish Socialist Party. The younger members were largely from the student generation of the 1960s; Jacek Kuroń was slightly older. The ideas and activity were led by Kuroń and the younger generation.

KOR's members openly declared themselves, publishing their home addresses and phone numbers. Piotr Jaroszewicz, the Prime Minister, ridiculed the new group: "We can only laugh at them".

By mid-1977 Radio Free Europe estimated there were one thousand KOR activists and thousands of sympathisers. In April 1977 the state began a phase of serious repression, and the next month KOR activist Stanisław Pyjas, a student at Kraków University, was killed, probably by the police. A Students' Solidarity Committee (SKS) was founded independent of the state student front, SZSP, whose members had attempted to disrupt protests against the killing.

Politically KOR was dominated by the ideas of Kuroń and Michnik. Michnik believed that the attempts of Communist revisionists to reform the Party had ended, by 1968, in complete failure. And the attempts at constructive engagement with the state by church groups had also failed. Michnik wanted to link reform to movements from below. Politically Kuroń and Michnik were Social Democrats, but in a country without a parliament and with a government that continued to rule without legitimacy and with violence and the backing of outside force. The threat of Russian intervention limited what the Polish opposition thought it could do; they aimed for an "unceasing struggle for reforms... that will extend civil liberties... for partial changes rather than violent overthrow of the existing regime." The same force that they believed made revolution impossible (Soviet intervention) also limited what reforms were possible. Kuroń accepted that the Party's control of the state could not be challenged; Poland could not be taken out of the Soviet bloc.

Kuroń and Michnik thought that new society-wide movements could reach a stable agreement with the state. The state itself might be willing to accept 'help', they thought, in order to find an orderly way out of the crisis it faced. As the KOR campaign in defence of the victimised workers became broader and more effective the government changed course and, on 19 November 1976, declared KOR illegal. KOR meetings were raided and the state attempted (and failed) to raise workers' opposition to KOR by petitioning against KOR in the factories. The Party then attempted to remove the reason for agitation by announcing an amnesty. By May 1977 only five workers (three from Radom and two from Ursus) were still in jail.

Given the original aims of KOR had been largely met KOR transformed itself into a broader organisation, the Committee for Social Self Defence (Komitet Samoobrony Spolecznej, KSS), with the old acronym added at the end in quotes, KSS-„KOR". They defined their aim as supporting "all initiatives aimed at realising Human and Civil Rights."

Although the public face of KOR was open and legal KOR activists helped create an enormous number of samizdat publications. In April 1978 a Party meeting was told there were nineteen independent publications.

June 1976. The state used tanks and helicopters to repress the workers. In Radom (above), 100km south of Warsaw in central Poland, 20,000 people took to the streets. The workers were met with live ammunition, water cannon and tear gas. 200 were injured, over 600 arrested and nearly a thousand workers were sacked

In March 1977 the Movement for the Defence of Civil and Citizens' Rights (ROPCiO) was formed, a more conservative opposition than KOR. The Ministry of the Interior claimed there were twenty-six 'anti-socialist' organisations in September 1979. These groups included The Society for Academic Courses (TKN), better known as the "flying university," which ran uncensored courses in private homes. An alternative publishing house, NOWa, had published about a hundred titles by 1980, including translations of George Orwell and Gunter Grass.

Four regional peasant committees were founded.

The workers' voice

The workers at the Ursus tractor factory openly objected to the victimisations at the plant. In a letter dated 4 November 1976, 889 workers demanded the reinstatement, to their old posts, of the workers' victimised following the June events. 67 workers who had been tortured in police custody sent a letter to the Prosecutor General demanding an investigation into police brutality (*The origins of Democratization in Poland*, Michael Bernhard).

After June 1976 the state slowed the economy, switching production towards consumption in the domestic market. Subsidies continued, estimated at 70% of the retail price by 1977. Workers were hit by an 8% increase in their costs of living in 1978. Half of all families suffered a cut in real income. National income fell by 2% in 1979; industrial production by 5%. Poland's foreign debt stood at $18bn.

By the end of the 1970s the Polish economic crisis was acute and the state attempted to make the workers pay. Most Polish workers were on piece-rates which meant that when frequent stoppages occurred – because of loss of energy, lack of raw materials, or parts, especially from abroad – the workers were those to suffer.

In 1978 piece-rate quotas were increased. At some of the shipyards workers were working 350 hours per month. Managers also manipulated quotas to reduce wages.

In industry there was widespread neglect of health and safety. *Robotnik* (*The Worker* bulletin) reported in 1978 that 2.8 million Poles worked in unsafe conditions. 50% of the women textile workers in Łódź had hearing problems due to noise levels. On the coast eight workers died building a ship. In 1978 KSS-„KOR" estimated that 180 miners died in accidents.

Health benefits were reduced to such an extent that only 15% of the monies collected for health were spent.

And the government, unable through fear of the working class to increase prices openly increased them surreptitiously by re-packaging goods. A new type of shop, a "commercial shop" sold meat marked up at 40-80% of the normal price.

Plans for a KSS-„KOR" publication, *Robotnik*, were made in August 1977. The title was taken from a turn-of-the-century underground paper of the old Polish Socialist Party. *Robotnik*'s stated goals were: "solidarity in defence of workers' interests; support of independent workers' representatives to replace the dead institutions of trade unions." *Robotnik* was consciously trying to create worker-intellectual cooperation to create "a just and independent Poland."

41

The first issue of 400 copies was four pages, printed on stencil duplicators. The aim was to publish bi-monthly. By issue nine the print run was 3000. Later their print technology improved allowing six typed pages to be reduced onto one printed sheet; the print run went up to 10-20,000 copies.

Activists estimated that each copy was read by between three and five workers. Meaning each issue produced after the summer of 1978 reached 30-100,000 workers. Each of the four issues published in July and August 1980 had a print run of 40,000. And *Robotnik* No. 60, printed at the end of August 1980, ran to 70,000 copies.

Robotnik developed a highly efficient distribution system, with fifty distribution centres across Poland. The highest proportion of bulletins went to Gdańsk (15-25%) and Warsaw (10%). *Robotnik* No. 35 contained a Charter of Workers' Rights, effectively the first draft of the 21 point charter Solidarność was to demand from the government in August 1980. This issue went through at least three printings between August and December 1979 and at least 100,000 copies were produced in total, going into all major industrial centres in the country. The Charter was signed by over one hundred activists, mainly skilled workers.

The Charter listed many general grievances and proposed some concrete solutions.

• Wages: linking of wages to the cost of living; a minimum wage; abolition of unjustified wage differentials; uniform wage scales across each industry.

• Hours: an end to forced overtime; a specified number of free Saturdays for all workers.

• Privilege: an end to privileges for Party and police officials particularly in distribution of apartments, land, cars, medical care, holidays and pensions.

The key demand, however, was for independent trade unions. The Charter stated that reforms had been won in the past but unless the workers had their own organisations capable of overseeing implementation of agreements, and protecting their representatives from victimisation, the state and managers would cheat them. The Charter made a number of suggestions, including that workers found their own Free Trade Union committees. And a fund for workers victimised for free trade union activity was founded.

The signatories insisted they were acting legally, in line with ILO conventions which the Polish government had signed in 1956, and the Polish constitution. Those allowed for free trade unions and the right to strike.

Free Trade Union committees were set up in three areas – Szczecin, Silesia and, most successfully, in Gdańsk. The Gdańsk organisation, the Committee for Free Trade Unions on the Coast (KZ-WZZ-W) took shape around the workers Andrzej Gwiazda and Joanna Duda-Gwiazda and an intellectual from Sopot, Bogdan

Borusewicz. The Gwiazdas' flat was used as an organising centre for KOR in the Gdańsk area.

Borusewicz had become one of the first editors of *Robotnik*, and his name and address had been printed in the second edition, in October 1977. In February 1978 police broke up an organising meeting in Borusewicz's flat by firing teargas into the apartment. In May a *Robotnik* meeting was raided by the secret police and nine people detained. As a result Błażej Wyszkowski was sentenced by a tribunal to two months in jail. He began a 33 day hunger strike and student and worker activists issued 15,000 copies of a leaflet protesting against the detention.

The Committee was able to withstand serious harassment – beatings, arrests, police infiltration — because of the widespread support the opposition carried amongst the working class. The Committee's members circulated *Robotnik* and supplemented it, later, with their own paper, *Worker of the Coast* (*Robotnik Wybrzeża*). Both sheets were read by several thousand workers in the Tri-city area. Although the quality of *Robotnik Wybrzeża* was high, and it was dedicated to examination of local issues, the print run might not have exceeded 300.

The Committee on the Coast pledged itself to help educate worker activists. Beginning in September 1978 self-education groups were set up. By the time the strikes of August 1980 began between one and two hundred workers had completed courses which included legal rights, dealing with the police and how to run a strike. *Robotnik* and other publications consciously allowed worker activists to discuss the lessons from past events.

KZ-WZZ-W also began to organise commemorations in the memory of those workers killed in the December 1970 massacre. Alongside ROPCiO and the student SKS, and KSS-„KOR" the local *Robotnik* group worked to build an event on 16 December 1977. Despite threats from the management at the Lenin yard and the State 1,000 people — 900 workers and 100 students — laid a wreath near Gate 2, the site of the murders. The next year, on 18 December 1978 4000 attended a similar ceremony despite a round-up of 28 activists in the run up.

In December 1979 200 people were detained in an attempt to stop the event, which 5-7,000 people attended. Speeches were made by Lech Wałęsa, and a cleric, Father Bronisław Sroka. Wałęsa had gone into hiding so he could be sure to attend.

Maryla Płońska, a tenants' activist, spoke for KZ-WZZ-W and stressed the need for working-class solidarity in defence of working-class representatives. Ceremonies attended by thousands were also held in Kalisz, Kraków, Poznań, Warsaw, Wrocław and Szczecin.

KZ-WZZ-W activists began being systematically victimised after December 1979. Firings or transfers in Gdańsk, at the end of the 70s, were often met with strikes to defend the activists. Joanna Duda-Gwiazda said later, "The general principle … was that until [workers] learned to defend their leaders against repression there would always be very few such people… [by] leaders I meant those who will be brave enough to openly, officially oppose the foreman, the management, on a definite issue."

On 16 December 1979 workers in W-2 and W-4 sections of the Lenin yard in Gdańsk held short strikes in defence of workmates who had been detained. W-2 struck on 31 December and 31 January 1980 in defence of the well-known activist, Anna Walentynowicz, who was being transferred. Lech Wałęsa led action in the Elektromontaż against sackings of those involved in the commemoration.

Importantly, for the shape of the events that were to come in 1980, the late 1970s saw an emerging alliance of the political, working-class opposition and the Church. Catholic intellectuals participated in KOR initiatives and the opposition received encouragement from the Catholic hierarchy. Cardinal Stefan Wyszyński encouraged the opposition to "defend the cultural values of the nation."

In June 1979 the newly installed Pope, John Paul II, the 59 year-old former Archbishop of Kraków, visited Poland for nine days. It was a triumphant procession through the country, witnessed directly by six million devout Poles, during which John Paul obliquely criticised Communist rule, the subjugation of Poland to the USSR and the lack of freedom for the Church. The contrast between the vastly popular Pope and the unpopular regime was clear.

The August events, 1980

Edward Babiuch, the Prime Minister, announced a plan to eliminate Poland's massive trade deficit by the end of 1980. Exports were to rise by 25% and supplies to home stores were to be cut by 15%. The Party intended to raise food prices, unannounced, bit by bit, starting on 1 July. But that did not save them. Workers at the Ursus tractor plant and the massive Huta Warszawa steelworks stopped work.

The authorities had decided to ride out any protests by immediately conceding pay rises to compensate for the price hike. The striking tractor and steel workers went back after getting 10% pay increases. On 11 July managers of major plants were summoned to Warsaw to be told to settle any disputes quickly. In fact the policy had the effect of encouraging strikes as workers quickly knew that any action would immediately win pay rises.

The official media was silent, but the BBC in London and the US-government funded, Munich-based Radio Free Europe reported on the strike wave. Jacek Kuroń, helped by a student of English from the Kraków group, coordinated information from a single phone in his Warsaw flat, and passed it on to the Western radio stations who then broadcast the news back into the country.

By the end of July workers in 68 enterprises had stopped work. Wage increases granted in July and early August stood at $1.1bn. The most dangerous strikes had taken place at Lublin in south east Poland, where rail and other transport workers had brought the city of 300,000 to a standstill for three days. The army had been used to deliver milk and bread.

Gierek had met Soviet leader Brezhnev in Crimea in late July. Gierek stayed in the USSR and went on holiday, and was still there when the Gdańsk strikes started on Thursday 14 August. Earlier that day Babiuch had looked out of his window to see Warsaw at a standstill. The bus drivers, who he thought had settled, were back out on strike and had been joined by the tram workers.

Nevertheless, no one had a clue about what was to start in Gdańsk.

The area round Gdańsk Bay held 800 factories employing over half a million workers. At the centre of industrial life was the Lenin shipyard with 17,000 workers and dozens of workshops spread over three square km, divided into two parts by a waterway, and connected by a single bridge. The Lenin shipyard had been founded in 1946 on the site of German yards which had been partially destroyed during the war.

45

The Free Trade Union group had tried and failed to get a strike in July against the price rises. They were pessimistic about their chances in August. But the week before the strike a number of members of the group met at Piotr Dyk's flat, in Wrzeszcz, just north of Gdańsk. Dyk was a member of Young Poland and they were meeting to celebrate the release of two political prisoners. Bogdan Borusewicz; Lech Wałęsa; Andrzej Gwiazda; Alina Pienkowska, a young nurse; Bogdan Felski, a 23-year-old from the Lenin yard; and Andrzej Kołódźiej a 20-year-old who had been fired from the Lenin yard; decided to call a strike in defence of Anna Walentynowicz who had been sacked that day. They went out into the courtyard, worried that Dyk's flat was bugged, and decided to call the strike the following week.

Anna Walentynowicz — Pani Anna, or Mrs Anna, as she was known — was a crane operator in the W-2 section, who had worked at the Lenin yard for thirty years, originally as a welder. She was in her early fifties, with thick glasses and hair in a bun, she was probably the most respected and the best speaker among the KZ-WZZ-W activists. She had been fired just a few months before she was due to retire; in the past few years she'd been harassed, transferred, warned, threatened. Now she was off sick.

But the Free Trade Union activists thought the workers might back her. They kept the strike date secret, even from other activists. In fact the original date they set for action had been Wednesday 13 August, but Lech Wałęsa had childcare responsibilities and the younger workers wanted him there, so the strike was put back a day.

In August 1980 Lech Wałęsa was a 37-year old electrician, and a good Catholic with six children living with his wife, Danuta, in a two room flat. He had been on the strike committee at the Lenin yard in December 1970 and had met Gierek in January 1971. Wałęsa had been sacked in 1976 for his involvement with the underground opposition. He later found work repairing machinery, but was dismissed again in January 1979; he was hired by Elektromontaż and sacked again in January 1980.

The week before the strike Wałęsa had been detained again, in front of his flat, while pushing his baby in a pram. The police had taken him and left the child alone in the street for a neighbour to find. He claimed to have been detained one hundred times between 1976 and 1980. Wałęsa possessed an acute sense of the mood of the workers around him and an ability to respond and to lead them. He saw himself as a man full of anger and an "uncouth man".

Early on the morning of Thursday 14 August Borusewicz led a team leafletting for the strike for Walentynowicz, meeting the trams and trains that dropped workers coming from the north. Another team met trains coming from the south.

By 5:45am Jerzy Borowczak had gathered 20 or 30 workers round him in the locker room of K-5, a small workshop on the far side of the yard. They had leaflets and posters advocating Anna Walentynowicz's reinstatement and a 1,000 złoty pay rise to cover the price increases. Some of the older workers were worried – they had families and were not sure the strike would succeed. About 30 workers started to march through the yard calling on others to follow them. In W-3 Bogdan Felski and two of his mates had posters up. About 50 workers were around him when the Division's director demanded to know what was going on. The Department's Party secretary turned up and tried to grab the banner the workers had made, but he was pushed back.

About 100 workers were marching now, demanding that others join them. Some did, some just watched and waited. The workers went past the electricians' section, W-4, and two old friends of Lech Wałęsa's, Stanislaw Bury and Henryk Lenarciak — both of whom had been active in the strikes of 1970 and 1976 — began to organise their Department. As the protest got to K-3 and K-1 there were 2,000 marchers. And a cheer went up.

They marched through every Department once again, now the crowd may have been as big as 8,000. As they passed the main gate, Gate 2, there was a moment when it looked as if the workers would surge through and into the town. The Free Trade Union people stopped that by asking for a minute's silence for those killed in 1970. The KOR people wanted an occupation, not another riot, precisely to avoid a repeat of 1970. The leaders moved the crowd a hundred metres into the shipyard, into the big square.

Klemens Gniech, the Director confronted them, and Jerzy Borowczak told him they were striking for Anna Walentynowicz but they would only speak to him later, after their meeting. To constitute the strike committee Borowczak took a list of twenty Department reps on a scrap of paper. From the top of a bulldozer Gniech attempted to get the workers back to work, saying negotiations could begin when work restarted. As he spoke Lech Wałęsa was climbing over the four metre high perimeter fence. Workers were drifting away when Wałęsa clambered onto the bulldozer and tapped Gniech on the shoulder. "Remember me?" he asked the boss. Wałęsa spoke briefly and announced an occupation. Many of the workers remembered Wałęsa from when he worked at the yard and others had heard him speak at the commemoration meeting in December; Wałęsa asked the workers if they would accept him on their strike committee. The workers roared their approval and a strike committee was set up, now with 21 members. They went to the canteen in W-4 to formulate their demands.

The committee refused to negotiate until Anna Walentynowicz was with them and demanded the Director's car was sent to pick her up.

Early that morning Anna Walentynowicz had been at the shipyard's health centre, outside the shipyard, a couple of blocks away from the main gate. Walentynowicz tried to phone Kuroń in Warsaw but the telephone operator was too afraid to put the call through. The yard's phones were cut and Walentynowicz's friend and fellow activist, Alina Pienkowska, who worked at the clinic, put the call through to Kuroń later that morning.

Pienkowska, a 27 year-old widow with a young child, then went down to the yard. Discovering no one had organised food for the workers she put out an appeal via the local radio then organised students to canvass the local area, spreading word about the occupation and looking for supplies.

Walentynowicz was determined to get inside the yard. There had been a strike in her defence in January that had fizzled out in because she was not able to get into the shipyard which had allowed the manager to persuade the workers to return to work. First she had to get rid of the four plainclothes police that were trailing her. She lost them by running from a Department store, across tram lines, and then into a friend's apartment. She could see the puzzled police, outside, through a crack in the curtains.

Eventually Walentynowicz was tracked down and delivered to the Lenin yard in the Director's Fiat Lada. A workers' militia was set up to take charge of all security at the yard. The militia's first act was to enforce a ban on vodka. In 1980 there were one million alcoholics in Poland and, apparently, 40% of all alcohol was consumed at work.

Early on Friday morning Andrzej Kołódźiej left the Lenin yard where he had been sacked in January and went to work at his new job at the Paris Commune Shipyard in Gdynia which employed 10,000 workers. Kołódźiej went from brigade to brigade, especially talking to the young workers. He told them the Lenin yard was on strike and they should stop work too. He was 20 years old and had only been working there for one day, after having lied — to get the job — about the reason he had been sacked from the Lenin yard.

The Paris Commune workers were tempted, but not convinced. Later that morning he saw a group forming in the shipyard square. The atmosphere was very tense. Someone had cut the electricity. Very quickly a crowd of 2,000 formed. Kołódźiej stopped the workers heading to meet the management and persuaded them to discuss their demands first.

At the Elmor factory the 2,000 workers were quickly organised to strike under a 36-member elected committee led by Gwiazda and a Party member, 27-year-old Bogdan Lis. Next door to the Lenin yard about a fifth of the workers were Party members and many were striking; although Lis was the only one to join the strike leadership. By mid-morning the tram and bus workers were on strike; 9,000 at

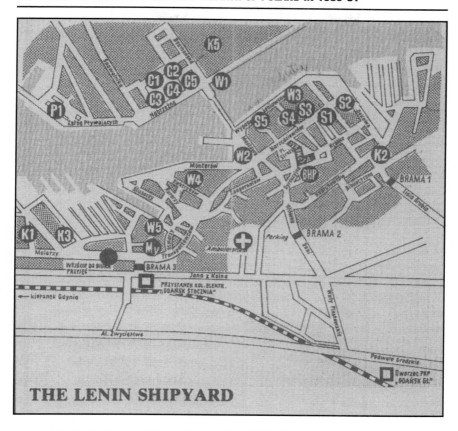

THE LENIN SHIPYARD

A map of the Lenin shipyard, Gdańsk, showing the individual workshops. The yard was divided in two by a waterway, the two sides connected by a single bridge.

At the bottom of the map the three gates are marked; brama translates as gate

Remontow and 4,000 workers at the Northern shipyards were out.

By mid-day 50,000 in the Tri-city ports area were on strike.

Inside the Lenin yard talks were beginning in the Health and Safety Centre, broadcast over the yard's PA system so every worker could hear. Director Gniech started by proposing the strike committee should be enlarged to represent all Divisions in the yard. Wałęsa reluctantly agreed and negotiations were suspended for a few hours while every Division elected four representatives. The new 150-strong committee assembled in the afternoon and now included management supporters and less militant workers from some of the less active sections. Then Gniech agreed to a wage hike, reinstatement for sacked workers, a monument for those killed in 1970, no reprisals.

Delegations from other factories started to arrive, converging on the Lenin yard as the biggest strike centre.

But by Saturday there was one only sticking point. The Lenin workers were holding out for a 2,000 złoty rise. Gniech agreed to 1,500, and the strike committee quickly voted to settle. It was three in the afternoon and Gniech demanded Wałęsa announce the end of the strike. Wałęsa did so, trying to make the best of it. Management got onto the works radio and demanded the yard be cleared. Workers began streaming out.

Outside the health centre there was utter confusion. The rep from Remontow started yelling at Wałęsa that the Gdańsk yard had betrayed them. Henryka Krzywonos, the woman who led the bus and tram workers, shouted at Wałęsa, "If you abandon us, we'll be lost. Buses can't face tanks." Alina Pienkowska went to Gate 3 and got the militia to shut the gates. She started appealing to the workers to stay put. Some of the women outside the yard, angry, spat at and jeered the workers who were leaving.

Wałęsa, sensing the mood, spoke to the crowd outside. Did they want the strike to continue? Yes, they shouted, they did. Wałęsa declared the strike would continue as a solidarity strike. The PA system was now shut down and so Wałęsa and Walentynowicz went round the yard on an electric trolley spreading the word through a megaphone.

The strike had been on a knife-edge and would have collapsed without the very small numbers of worker activists, organised in advance, with clear aims, and with respect based on a history of struggle among the broader mass of workers. In fact the strike would not have started without their actions and planning.

By 5 o'clock there were only about 1,500 workers left inside, mostly militant younger workers. But that evening the strike rose to a new level as delegates from 21 striking enterprises declared the Inter-factory Strike committee (Międzyzakładowy Komitet Strajkowy, MKS). Joanna and Andrzej Gwiazda, Bogdan Lis and Bogdan Borusewicz worked on a set of demands. Their original 16 demands reached a completed form on Sunday evening after being debated by the MKS delegates.

The final 21 Demands were an enormous step forward for the working-class opposition of Eastern Europe. However, various demands – such as the call for free elections – were not included. The Demands implicitly accepted certain limits on the movement's aspirations. The questions of completely abolishing censorship and free elections had been deliberately omitted; Bogdan Borusewicz commented: "You know what happened when they abolished censorship in Czechoslovakia in 1968."

After 8am on Sunday morning, 17 August, people started arriving from the town. The gates were decked out with flowers and portraits of John Paul II. Over 5,000 people attended mass at 9am.

Management then attempted to break the strike by pitting those inside the yard against the workers who were coming in on Monday morning. Before 6am Gniech used the PA system to tell the workers the strike had been settled on Saturday. Wałęsa made a patriotic speech to the workers. They sang a hymn. The workers outside the gate were still undecided, some were hostile. The gates were open and a young worker shouted, "If you think you're a real shipyard worker, then come in." A group of thirty younger workers broke ranks and walked in, many followed. Strikers on both sides of the entrance burst into applause.

Across Poland the importance of Gdańsk was being felt. Szczecin is a town of 400,000 in north west Poland. 55,000 worked in shipbuilding, including 12,000 at the Warski yard. On Saturday 16 August – unexpectedly — the entire workforce got a 10% pay increase.

Work began as normal on Monday but by mid-morning a mass meeting had convened and decided to elect delegates from each department and discuss the events. A strike was called. Soon word came that the Parnica yard and Gryfia repair yard had stopped work too. The Warski workers elected a committee led by Marian Jurczyk, a strike leader from 1970, and produced a list of 36 demands of their own. At 8pm the workers listened through car radios and the PA systems of occupied workplaces as Gierek addressed the nation. He offered money but rejected all the strikers' political demands. A groan went round the Lenin yard as Gierek told them there was already freedom to criticise in Poland.

By that evening 263 enterprises had sent delegates to the MKS. A delegation had turned up at the Lenin yard from Elblag, a city 50km from Gdańsk closer to the Soviet border. An MKS had been formed in Elblag.

Having tried to settle with the Lenin yard and failed the government then tried to settle with other enterprises. The state issued a statement which claimed it had reached agreement with workers' committees from seventeen enterprises. The government's representative, Tadeusz Pyka said a deal had been reached on over twenty issues including maternity leave, a pay rise of 1,500 złoty, Saturday working and health and housing. By the evening the government's strategy was coming apart as the workers in the seventeen factories arrived in the Lenin yard. Delegates from the Techmor and Klimor plants told the MKS that Pyka had struck a deal with their factory bosses and the factory Party secretary, not the workers' representatives.

In Warsaw a dozen KOR members were arrested, including Kuroń and Michnik. And a barrage of propaganda appeared in the press accusing the strikers of undermining the national economy.

The strikes were spreading. The Nowa Huta steel plant near Kraków struck for two hours in solidarity. A delegation of miners from Lower Silesia arrived at the Lenin yard at 4pm. The MKS now represented committees at 304 enterprises. 64 prominent Warsaw intellectuals issued an appeal: "The crisis arrived... [as] a result of broken promises, of all the attempts to suppress the crisis, of disregard for civil rights... It is impossible to rule the Polish nation without listening to its voice... Polish workers are fighting for a better and more dignified life. The place of all progressive intelligentsia is on the side of the workers."

Timothy Garton Ash reports an interesting incident which took place on Thursday 21 August. Ireneusz Leśniak from the personnel department demanded to speak during the workers' discussions in the Lenin hall. He read a statement which lasted ten minutes. He asked for Gierek to come to the yard, describing Gierek as "like the Pope". And said, "Edward Gierek, who alone we trust, because you are to us like a father." Garton Ash comments, "Astonishingly, the delegates crowned the peroration with resounding applause.

"Then Anna Walentynowicz took the microphone: 'I know Mr Leśniak,' she said, 'I know him because he has persecuted me for years — it was he who sacked me two weeks ago.' Suddenly the hall was on its feet, delegates who a moment before had applauded so vigorously now crowded around the white-faced Leśniak on the podium, fists raised, threatening to lynch him. Wałęsa seized the microphone, shouted for calm, and then personally escorted Leśniak through the now silent crowd to the gate."

Garton Ash comments that the crowd of 600 workers had revealed something: "how unclear many [MKS] delegates were about their strategy and goals."

By Friday 22 August 200,000 workers were on strike along the Baltic coast. The Gdańsk MKS included 350 workplace delegates and the Szczecin Inter-factory Committee included over sixty enterprises. At many smaller industrial centres across northern Poland work had also stopped. The government was still reluctant to recognise the MKS as an entity they would negotiate with. But later that day they began to talk.

30,000 copies of the first edition of a strike bulletin were printed. KOR activist Konrad Bieliński, who worked for the samizdat publisher NOWa, began production. The bulletin stated, "The news in the press, radio and television is both distorted and incomplete. The whole country awaits genuine and accurate news from the strike-bound Baltic coast... the strike action is coordinated by the demo-

Anna Walentynowicz (1929-2010), top left; Lech Wałęsa (born 1943), top right; Alina Pienkowska (1952-2002), bottom left; Andrzej Gwiazda (born 1935), bottom right

cratically elected MKS… A false impression is being created that the workers in public services have not joined the strike. In fact, they joined us very early, but continue to maintain essential services with the full consent of the MKS… Our demands are completely within the law and in no way in conflict with the existing system or the government's political alliances." In other words the MKS was saying they did not intend to threaten the PZPR's grip on power, nor the relationship with the USSR.

Saturday 23 August. At 8pm the government and Party delegation arrived at the Lenin yard by bus. As their bus nudged through the crowd the workers drummed on the side. As the state's team got off the bus one thousand workers stared at them.

Deputy Prime Minister Mieczysław Jagielski faced the union delegation across the formica table. One wall was glass and dozens of press people from all over the world were looking in. The MKS delegates sat facing the Party bosses. Jagielski was dressed in a good suit and looked like a Western banker. To Jagielski's left was Zbigniew Zieliński who, "stands out by virtue of his grossness. Fat-faced, pot-bellied, grunting [Zieliński] looks like a caricature of a corrupt communist functionary. Directly opposite him sits Andrzej Gwiazda, founding father of the Free Trades Unions on the Coast, with the bearded, emaciated face of an El Greco saint and memories of a life-long struggle that began in Siberia [he and his mother were deported by the Soviets in 1940; his father had been imprisoned by the Nazis]. These two faces tell of two worlds, and two moralities, which now confront each other across the table." (*The Polish Revolution*, Timothy Garton Ash).

Jagielski talked to the workers "as if he was talking to children". What he said was broadcast across the shipyard. One audience was the MKS members who were crammed in the hall. Beyond the delegates were the Lenin workers listening in the yard. And beyond the gate were hundreds of women workers. Jagielski declared that the strikes were breaking the economy. He said the Polish bureaucrats enjoy no privileges and — to audible sighs and muttering — that there were no political prisoners in Poland.

The MKS delegation insisted that a precondition to talks continuing was that the phone connections that had been cut, separating Gdańsk from the rest of the country, were restored. Zieliński declared that a hurricane had destroyed the Warsaw phone exchange the previous night. It was explained to Zieliński that the phone lines were cut on 15 August, a week before the "hurricane".

The Party, in crisis, reshuffled itself, with Gierek's supporters losing out and the hardliner, Stefan Olszowski, brought back from East Germany. The Party meeting was shown concluding, on television; inside the yard, as the PZPR leaders sang the Internationale, the workers rose to sing the national anthem.

Behind the scenes other, private, negotiations took place. The Party was looking for a deal.

Significantly, Tadeusz Mazowiecki, one of the intellectuals brought in to help the union, suggested a "compromise" on independent unions. He proposed a fall-back position, democratisation of the existing state-run unions. The MKS rejected the idea. The workers knew what they wanted, and they knew their own independent force was the only guarantee they had that they would not be cheated by the state. They had been cheated before. The workers had already gone far

The Solidarność logo was created by the artist Jerzy Janiszewski.

Janiszewski joined the Gdańsk shipyard occupation in August 1980. He chose red paint for Poland's history and the blood that had been split in past workers' protests. The merged letters were for unity and solidarity.

He printed a few hundred copies of his design on an improvised press and they were plastered round the shipyard

beyond what some of the pro-worker intelligentsia thought was possible; the intellectuals tended to hold the movement back.

Bronisław Geremek and Mazowiecki had arrived on 22 August with a message of support from 62 Warsaw intellectuals. The strike committee had asked them to help advise the workers on the negotiations.

On Tuesday 26 August, the thirteenth day of occupation, members of the workers' defence guard linked arms to allow the state's delegation peacefully into the yard. Wałęsa opened by declaring, "We do not want to disturb the principles of social ownership of the means of production. We consider our factories to be the property of the Polish nation, but we demand that we should be the real masters in the factory and in the country." Jagielski said the government promised, in some cases, to respect the right to strike. Wałęsa and Gwiazda demanded the right to free trade unions, stating that this was more important than every other demand. Gwiazda talked about the existing unions, which "did not defend [the workers'] interests, but on the contrary accommodated management, all the time ready to act hand-in-hand with management against the workers' interests." He said the state unions could remain, but new independent ones should be permitted. He then went on to discuss the freedom to speak, demanding that workers should have the right to publish: "It is necessary that [we are able] to write the truth, irrespective of whether or not this truth suits the current leadership…

Workers have to have freedom of speech when they are right *and* when they are wrong. Discussion is possible only when there are opinions which are not considered in advance to be the 'correct' opinions." The atmosphere outside the room was electric and loud cheering was heard inside the hall after Gwiazda concluded.

The discussion was left to a smaller committee while delegates in the hall heard that the miners in Wrocław had declared an MKS, the fourth. In Wrocław 30 factories employing 30,000 workers were striking. That night the aging Cardinal Wyszyński spoke on television, preaching "peace, calm, reason, prudence and responsibility for the Polish nation." The Church was helping the regime. In the Lenin yard the workers' reaction was of disappointment; the devout Lech Wałęsa tried to shrug off the Cardinal's attempt to hold back the workers' movement. The next morning's paper, *Trybuna Ludu*, warned of a catastrophe which — in a thinly veiled threat — could lead to a Russian invasion.

On Wednesday 27 August 500 enterprises were on strike in and around Gdańsk. Strikes had begun in Bydgoszcz and Torun, industrial centres south of Gdańsk. A car factory in Bielsko-Biała was out; the bus workers had struck in Kraków. The Nowa Huta steel workers were drawing up a list of demands.

In Gdańsk a series of discussions had begun behind the main scene involving small groups from each side. On the workers' side each group had three members of the intelligentsia on hand to advise them. There was interesting testimony from the sociologist, Jadwiga Staniszkis, about this process. Staniszkis was there to help the workers' team but she was alarmed by this backroom process of negotiation which proceeded in a friendly manner because – in her view – the six intellectuals were all from the same Warsaw social circles. She regarded the "internal loyalty" among the intellectuals to be a danger for the workers, a snare. Certainly the middle-class advisers played a temporising role throughout Solidarność's existence.

The workers and the bureaucrats both understood the centrality of the demand for free trade unions. The government side declared, "Your demand for independent unions has become an ideological precedent." The government wanted the text to include an explicit recognition of the Party's "leading role."

On the morning of Thursday 28 August the questions of censorship and political prisoners were debated. The author, Lech Bądkowski, white-haired and in his 50s, stopped short of demanding the abolition of censorship but demanded legal guarantees to allow free expression and the truthful provision of information. Andrzej Gwiazda, living under intense pressure and with little sleep, spoke about the student victimisations of 1968 and the sackings which followed the strikes of 1970 and 1976. He asked, "Mr Premier, this is the key issue: Are we going to live in a democratic system or a police state? People are afraid, even to speak out. And this has to be done away with." Outside the gates, listening to Gwiazda over loud-speakers, his words were passionately received by thousands of workers. Wałęsa was charismatic and passionate, but Gwiazda got to the point.

Jagielski appeared close to concluding an agreement in Gdańsk, but from Warsaw the Central Committee's ideological department warned of "anti-social-ist" elements amongst the strikers. That warning was echoed in the national press. The ideological department reckoned that independent unions would "have the practical function of an opposition party... They would give birth to a situation of dual power." They were right.

On Friday 29 further detentions of Warsaw dissidents took place as commis-sions worked in the background on the details of an agreement. Strengthening the workers' position 20,000 Silesian copper miners joined the Baltic coast strikers. A delegate from Silesia – in Gierek's backyard – arrived at the Lenin yard with a message of solidarity. The country was close to a general strike. Inside the Politburo the hard-liner, Stefan Olszowski, was arguing that a "state of war" should be declared; he was opposed by Jaruzelski (Defence) and Kania (Internal Security). Jagielski was instructed to settle with the strikers, peacefully, as quickly as possible.

On Saturday 30 August a large banner was hung from the shipyard walls, "Proletarians of all factories, Unite!" Jagielski appeared calm as Wałęsa opened the new round of talks in the glassed-in conference room. Point 1 of the agreement began: "To accept trade unions as free and independent of the party" and con-tained seven subsections. The first read: "The activity of the trade unions in People's Poland has not lived up to the hopes and aspirations of the workers. We thus consider that it will be beneficial to create new union organisations, which will run themselves, and which will be authentic expressions of the working class." The document added that the old unions would continue to exist.

In return the workers conceded to the Party that the new unions would not constitute a political party and "will recognise the leading role of the PZPR in the state and will not oppose the existing system of international alliances."

Jagielski wanted progress, quickly, and the further points of the agreement were run through in outline. He told the meeting he would go to Warsaw to get authority to sign the deal and would return later that day. He wanted work to start again almost immediately. Wałęsa declared work would start again on Monday. "And one more thing," Wałęsa demanded. "Arresting KOR members should stop. If they start doing something wrong, we'll stop them ourselves." Jagielski said he would look into it.

As Jagielski left arguments broke out about the concessions the union had made to the Party. Some workers argued the acceptance of the Party's 'leading role' was a betrayal. Mazowiecki, the adviser, tried to smooth over the issue. Wałęsa answer the charge directly, "It would be better without it. But it was necessary and we must all understand that."

Wałęsa then proposed the MKS issue an ultimatum to the government demanding the release of the arrested KOR activists. The demand was accepted by acclaim and Wałęsa had the unity of the conference room around him again.

Father Jankowski led the 9am mass outside the gates on Sunday morning, 31 August. The crowd was enormous. The final round of talks began at 11.30am. Gwiazda broke into the discussion to ask Jagielski about the list of detainees he had provided. Jagielski hedged. Walentynowicz then named Mirosław Chojecki, head of the opposition printing organisation, NOWa, saying, "He's in jail now." Wałęsa said: "If they are not released we will strike again."

As the two sides resumed their meeting at 4.30pm, preparing to sign the agreement that would end the strike and legalise the free trade unions, Wałęsa asked about the KOR prisoners. Jagielski declared that the prosecutor's office would make a decision by midday the following day, Monday 1 September.

As the MKS presidium and the government commission entered the jammed conference hall the television lights came on. It was 5 o'clock and millions of Poles watched on television.

Lech Wałęsa, true to himself and his beliefs, ended the strike: "We go back to work on 1 September. We all know what this day reminds us of [the Nazi invasion of 1939]. About the Motherland, about the national cause, about the common interests of the family whose name is Poland... Have we achieved everything we wanted? Frankly, no, not everything but... we've achieved a lot... we have the most important thing: our independent self-governing trade unions. This is our guarantee for the future... I proclaim the strike to be over."

The two sides signed off the 21 points filed in a blue plastic binder. Wałęsa used in a foot-long red-and-white pen, a souvenir of the Pope's visit.

The proud and glorious Polish working class had won the right to free and independent union organisations. The events of August and the workers' victory was the greatest single act by a working class against a bureaucratic Stalinist ruling class that the world had ever seen. The next stage of the struggle had begun.

Signing the Gdańsk agreement, 31 August 1980. Standing, left, Deputy Prime Minister, Mieczysław Jagielski (1924-97), and, on the right, Lech Wałęsa

The 21 Demands

1. Acceptance of free trade unions independent of the Communist Party and of enterprises, in accordance with convention No. 87 of the International Labour Organisation concerning the right to form free trade unions.

2. A guarantee of the right to strike and of the security of strikers.

3. Compliance with the constitutional guarantee of freedom of speech, the press and publication, including freedom for independent publishers, and the availability of the mass media to representatives of all faiths.

4. A return of former rights to: 1) People dismissed from work after the 1970 and 1976 strikes. 2) Students expelled because of their views. The release of all political prisoners, among them Edmund Zadrozynski, Jan Kozlowski, and Marek Kozlowski. A halt in repression of the individual because of personal conviction.

5. Availability to the mass media of information about the formation of the Inter-factory Strike Committee and publication of its demands.

6. Bringing the country out of its crisis situation by the following means: a) making public complete information about the social-economic situation. b) enabling all social classes to take part in discussion of the reform programme.

7. Compensation of all workers taking part in the strike for the period of the strike.

8. An increase in the pay of each worker by 2,000 złoty a month.

9. Guaranteed automatic increases in pay on the basis of increases in prices and the decline in real income.

10. A full supply of food products for the domestic market, with exports limited to surpluses.

11. The introduction of food coupons for meat and meat products (until the market stabilizes).

12. The abolition of commercial prices and sales for Western currencies in the so-called internal export companies.

13. Selection of management personnel on the basis of qualifications, not party membership, and elimination of privileges for the state police, security service, and party apparatus by equalization of family allowances and elimination of special sales, etc.

14. Reduction in the age for retirement for women to 50 and for men to 55, or (regardless of age) after working for 30 years (for women) or 35 years (for men).

15. Conformity of old-age pensions and annuities with what has actually been paid in.

16. Improvements in the working conditions of the health service.

17. Assurances of a reasonable number of places in day-care centres and kindergartens for the children of working mothers.

18. Paid maternity leave for three years.

19. A decrease in the waiting period for apartments.

20. An increase in the commuter's allowance to 100 złoty.

21. A day of rest on Saturday. Workers in the brigade system or round-the-clock jobs are to be compensated for the loss of free Saturdays with increased leave or other paid time off.

After August

On 1 September, carrying a bunch of gladioli and a wooden crucifix, Lech Wałęsa attempted to open the office of the new union. He was locked out. Eventually a caretaker was found who opened the door to a small, empty room. Wałęsa declared, "I am in an empty room, but one full of hope".

In Warsaw small groups of KOR activists were released, including Kuroń.

Down south in the Silesian coalfields eight men were killed by a runaway coal wagon. There was an explosion of anger and by 2 September 200,000 miners were on strike. An MKS headquarters was established at the Manifest Lipcowy mine in Jastrzebie near the Czech border. The coal and lignite the miners dug provided 85% of the country's fuel and 15% of its export earnings; they had a powerful position.

The Silesian workers refused to deal with the Minister of Mines and quickly signed a deal with the Deputy Premier, Aleksander Kopeć. The agreement began with a declaration that the miners "fully support the 21 demands advanced by the striking crews of the coast and, in particular, the point concerning trade unions." They also had their own concerns. They put an end to the hated "four-brigade" shift system which was designed to keep the pits working 24-hours a day, seven days a week, but meant that the miners worked most Sundays. They also won new health and safety rules.

On 5 September Gierek allegedly suffered a heart attack and was quickly removed as PZPR First Secretary and replaced by Stanislaw Kania. The government declared that the 10% pay rise awarded to 12 million state sector workers would cost 90bn złotys.

The Polish Politburo meeting of 4-5 October received a report which said in the period July – September 1980 strikes had taken place at 2000 enterprises involving 1.2m workers.

As Kania attempted to stabilise his rule, the new movement began to organise. On Wednesday 17 September representatives from 35 Inter-factory Committees and 150 large individual factories met in the Hotel Morski in Gdańsk for the first Independent Self-Governing Trade Union (NSZZ) national delegates' meeting. In two weeks three million workers from 3,500 factories had joined the new organisation, or one quarter of the non-agricultural workforce. The meeting decided to form a confederation of regional bodies coordinated by a National Commission (KKP) based in Gdańsk and led by Wałęsa.

The regional bodies, Inter-factory Committees (MKS), were themselves based on factory committees (KZ). The KKP was directed by delegates from the MKSs.

The new workers' movement debated its structure: "whether Solidarity should consist of a strong national central authority or a series of cooperating unions with a weak national body limited to advising virtually independent regional centres." The better-organised areas preferred strong regional bodies and a weak central structure believing the leaders would remain closer to the rank and file and there was less chance of a bureaucratised centre emerging. "Apparently Wałęsa wanted a weak central structure... Opposition, however, was heavy from representatives of small provincial industrial centres where Party officials and factory managers usually ruled dictatorially together. [This group]... favoured a strong central organisation that could come to their assistance." (Nicholas Andrews, *Poland 1980-81*)

Reports of intimidation in weaker areas were made. The old state-run unions were making propaganda saying workers would lose health and social security benefits if workers left the old unions. Solidarność organisers were being harassed, detained, denied premises and threatened. So, at a meeting in Gdańsk on 17 September representatives from the new unions decided that all unions affiliated to Solidarność would adopt the same statutes and register as one union.

As the old unions pulled out of the Stalinist Central Council of Trade Unions and began to register they also claimed to be "independent self-governing trade unions" or NSZZ. The real workers' movement appended the word "Solidarność" (Solidarity) to distinguish themselves, and this was the name they became known by.

The Party feared the collapse of the old state-run "unions" and formed a new organisation, the Coordinating Committee of Labour Unions, to try to save the remaining assets and structures of the state's labour fronts.

Wałęsa filed papers for Solidarność's registration on 28 September and declared a one-hour warning strike for Friday 3 October. The strike demanded that the authorities fulfil the obligations they had signed up to on pay rises and union recognition. At noon, with factory sirens sounding the start of the strike to the 11,000 workers at the Warsaw steelworks, Solidarność Chair, Seweryn Jaworski, marched through the plant with the strike committee, fists raised, shouting "No more lies! No more decisions about us, without us!" At thousands of selected enterprises Solidarność put on a disciplined show of force.

At the start of October rumours began to circulate that Solidarność's registration would not be recognised by the Warsaw court. Solidarność considered another strike. The Chief Judge attempted to explain the delay by saying the Solidarność's newly formulated statutes did not explicitly recognise the leading role of the Party, as was done in the Gdańsk agreement. The unions replied that the statutes were fine as the unions had already recognised the "socialist system" by signing in Gdańsk.

Solidarność's 34-member National Coordinating Commission (KKP) met the Prime Minister on 31 October in Warsaw. Some issues were resolved: the government gave Solidarność permission to publish a paper, to receive printing equipment sent from abroad and impounded by customs, and to get radio and television time. The date set for the Supreme Court to consider the union's registration was 10 November. As 10 November approached the tension rose and Solidarność discussed selective strikes from 12 November if registration failed. In fact the Supreme Court allowed registration without amending the main text of the union's statutes.

Alongside the workers, other groups were organising. Student activists demanding their own free students' union had held their first meeting in Gdańsk on 27 August. Over 18-19 October a national organisation was founded, the Independent Students' Association (NZS), at the University of Technology in Warsaw. The NZS saw itself as continuing the tradition of the Student Solidarity Committee formed after the murder of student KOR activist Stanisław Pyjas in Kraków in 1977.

The new organisation petitioned for legal recognition, which was denied by the courts in October 1980. Students began to organise strikes, sit-ins and occupations in support of their right to organise. Following mass actions the government agreed to recognise the Association in February 1981. The government also abolished compulsory Russian language courses and units in "Marxist-Leninism".

The first national NZS delegate meeting took place at the University of Kraków, 3-6 April 1981. 240 delegates from 66 colleges attended.

Opposition groups elsewhere in the Eastern Bloc were following the events in Poland closely. Charter 77 in Czechoslovakia issued a statement in support of Solidarność. Vladimir Klebanov's beleaguered Association of Free Trade Unions for Workers' Defence (SMOT), in the USSR, released an appeal in the West proposing a committee of free trade union activists across Eastern Europe. Hungarian oppositionists attempted to travel to Poland to show their sympathy with the new unions but were stopped at Budapest airport. And 20 oppositions in the Baltic states issued a letter, published in the West, in support of the free trade unions and democratic reforms.

Politics, the Party, intervention, and the "self-limiting revolution"

Solidarność emerged as a hybrid. Part union, part network of workers' councils and part political movement.

The first explicitly and entirely political strike began in late January 1981 in Bielsko-Biała near to the Czechoslovakian border. The strike was against the ostentatious corruption of the leading Party officials and appointees, following the completion of a 150-page report into fraud, theft and bribery amongst local and regional officials, including the stealing of 34 million złotys which had been collected locally to build a recreational arena for people in the area.

The strike's demands were for the removal of corrupt local officials. A one hour warning strike began on 26 January and the main strike took place from 27 January directed by the local MKS based on 54 large enterprises in the area. Factories were occupied and only essential services (some transport and hospitals) remained functioning; 200,000 workers took part.

The local Solidarność officials had not sought agreement from Solidarność's national leaders and the strike movement was initially opposed by Lech Wałęsa who tried to end it. However, faced with intransigent local activists, Wałęsa swung behind the strike, issuing a telex to Solidarność organisations across the country calling for a mass strike if violence was used against the Bielsko-Biała protesters. The movement ended on 5-6 February in a complete victory for the workers after the intervention of a delegation of Bishops sent by the Primate, Stefan Wyszyński. The Bishops had been asked to intervene by Wałęsa using the moderate Catholic intellectual and Solidarność adviser Tadeusz Mazowiecki as a go-between.

Party officials at Regional and local level as well as the local mayor of Bielsko-Biała and the Chief of Police were sacked or resigned.

The workers' militancy was rising. A regional general strike took place in the south-west town of Jelenia Gora on 9 February. The National Commission delegate from Poznań, Lech Dymarski, referred to the pressure on the KKP, "[The authorities] have no other purpose but to destroy … the union… The government has its back to the wall, but so do we. Our walls are the rank and file."

The workers' demand for an uncensored and truthful press had become acute. Since the August strikes official censorship had become much less thorough. Many Solidarność bulletins and papers had begun to spring up. The Gdańsk *Solidarity* and Warsaw *Independence* were both uncensored. By early May the Solidarność news agency, AS, listed 87 Solidarność journals and bulletins. 40-50,000 of Poland's print workers were Solidarność members and they struck against the censorship imposed on the Szczecin Solidarność paper, *Jednosc* (Timothy Garton Ash).

Solidarność did not base itself on a political party, nor did it create one. That was the conscious decision of the leading militants like Wałęsa who explicitly rejected the idea of forming an alternative party, and, in particular, of the intellectuals like Kuroń who opposed attempts to overthrow the state power in favour of a project of hollowing out that power, pushing the state back by creating a multitude of civil society institutions which would negotiate an accommodation with the state. Indeed these opposition groups would be able to negotiate a compromise with the state because — the intellectuals believed – the state would come to see that it could rule more effectively with the cooperation of the free trade unions and other independent organisations. This wishful thinking would be brutally exposed, later, in December 1981; at the time, however, these views were disorientating and disarming.

Kuroń's aim was for the Party to withdraw, only controlling the basic functions of national defence and police, leaving space for managers to run enterprises on the basis of real autonomy, according to ability, not party affiliation, which would allow Solidarność to become a "normal" Western-style trade union movement.

Jacek Kuroń first described Solidarność as a self-limiting movement, unable to engage in party politics, or aspire to overthrow the Stalinist government because of the threat of Soviet invasion. That general idea was very widely accepted by the rank and file of Solidarność because it was based on a very real threat of Soviet force. What was debated, however, were the boundaries that could not be crossed.

For the same reasons the deep rooted nationalist consciousness of the oppressed Polish people did not find an overt mass political voice for a struggle against the Soviet Union. The Nationalist KPN (Konfederacja Polski Niepodległej) advocated the fight for a "Third Polish Republic", but got little support. Before August 1980 it had organised protests which had involved a few thousand people. In August 1980 Leszek Moczulski and four other KPN leaders were arrested with other oppositionists. When Kuroń and the KOR leaders were released Moczulski stayed in jail and became a martyr.

Solidarność disagreed with Moczulski's views but petitioned for his release.

Moczulski's wife went on hunger strike and students and Young Poland organised street demonstrations – not a method of protest favoured by Solidarność – in support of Moczulski. Eventually the KPN people were released after Solidarność strike action in March 1981. Nevertheless, clear anti-USSR agitation was not popular; Solidarność activists were scared of its implications.

The conscious directing ideas which shaped Solidarność were those of the intellectuals from the secular and church opposition groups whose policy was to limit the movement's scope and to look for a compromise with the state. The Polish Stalinists' regime, aspiring to totalitarianism but never able to achieve it, had been forced to leave space for opposition. But the regime found the scale of the post-August opposition movement intolerable. The Stalinist state, which by its nature needed to exert direct control over every aspect of social organisation was incapable of existing alongside a ten-million-strong, militant workers' movement. There was dual power in Poland and the question was: who would prevail?

The Russians had used violence and terror against the Hungarian workers in 1956 and in Czechoslovakia in 1968. In December 1979 tanks had gone into Afghanistan to prop up a client state, and the threat of intervention was very real. It seems that in November-December 1980 the Russian Communists considered, and rejected, the idea of invading Poland. Kania had warned the Russians, already bogged down in Afghanistan, they would face a national rising and promised to deal with Solidarność internally. The Soviets were also wary of US reaction, which held them back.

The possibility of invasion was used as a means of Russian pressure on the forces inside the country, including the ruling Party.

The Party

To be a PZPR member was a route to possible power and privilege. Party members at work received better bonuses and jobs, access to bigger apartments and better education for their children. Party members occupied the 2-300,000 *nomenklatura* posts – a list of the network of key administrative and other state positions filled at the direction of the Party. This was the core of the Polish ruling class. If family members were included the Polish elite was probably about one and a half million strong, out of a population of 35m.

Despite purges and resignations following the crises in 1958-9, 1968, and again in 1971, the Party had grown from 1,368 million after unification with the purged Socialists in 1949, to 3,079 million in 1979. The Party members were 11.9% of the adult population; 46% were designated "workers"; 27% were women.

"Various estimates suggest that in January of 1981, between 1.4 and 1.7 million of the Party's three million members were also members of Solidarność. At the Party's Congress in July 1981, it was reported that 20% of the delegates were also Solidarność members." Solidarność did, however have a rule that stated no office holder in Solidarność could either hold office in the Communist Party or be an official of the state (councillor, magistrate etc); Solidarność was to be independent of the state.

An opinion poll conducted for Paris Match in late 1980 found that only 3% of the population would vote for the Communists in a free election.

Trust in the Party had evaporated: "A poll conducted by the Centre for Public Opinion Research showed the Catholic Church, Solidarność, and the army, in that order, as the most trusted institutions in Poland. At the very bottom of the list, in fifteenth place, was the Polish United Workers' Party. A similar poll conducted later among Solidarność members in the Mazowsze region showed a similar ranking: Solidarność had the confidence of 95% of the respondents; the Church, 93%; the Army, 68%. The Party, again at the bottom of a list of fourteen institutions, was trusted by only 7% of the respondents." (*Membership of the PZPR, D Mason*)

In such conditions the Party lost authority, members and self-confidence. In December 1980, at the Central Committee's Plenum, delegates estimated that up to 30% of members had stopped paying dues.

An opposition had emerged, centred on Party members in the university town of Torun, south of Gdańsk, seeking to link Party members 'horizontally' and to radically democratise the Party. Zbigniew Iwanow, a 32-year-old engineer at the Towimore marine engineering plant, a striker and Party member, had been elected Party Secretary at his factory. Iwanow set up a "horizontal" coordination, the Consultative Commission, of Party Secretaries from the surrounding area. In November Iwanow was expelled from the Party for "factionalism," however he carried on regardless, backed by a vote of confidence from his members. On 15 April 1981 750 delegates, claiming to represent one million Party members, met in Torun to plan for the democratisation of their Party in the run-up to the forthcoming Party Congress.

The Congress finally met in July 1981 and the reformers were defeated. Timothy Garton Ash explains the failure of the Party reform movement as being rooted in the lack of support in the country for reforming the Party: there was no mass drive to do so; worker members were reluctant to take up the struggle in the Party. That is true, no doubt. But the higher echelons of the Party were also the centres of political organisation for the bureaucratic ruling class, and they were not willing to give up so easily. On the conservative edge of the PZPR other forces began to organise. A group called the Grunwald Patriotic Union launched itself in March 1981 with a ceremony commemorating "victims of Zionist terror". On 15 May pro-Soviet conservatives in the Party, who called themselves the Katowice Forum, published an attack on Kania warning of "Trotskyite-Zionism, nationalism, clericalism and anti-Sovietism" and the possibility of a "liberal takeover" at the next Party Congress.

March 1981

One hundred and seventy kilometers south of Gdańsk is the town of Bydgoszcz. Bydgoszcz is at the centre of an agricultural area and was known for the production of cycles and mopeds.

Following the registration of Solidarność organisations of independent farmers had been pressing for the registration of Wiejska Solidarność (Rural Solidarity).

The local famer activists were involved in an occupation, backed by Solidarność, in support of registration. Following a long meeting with local councillors on 19 March about 45 activists were attacked and beaten by the Militia and secret police. Singled out was Jan Rulewski, a well-known militant on Solidarność's National Commission and a technician in his early 30s. Rulewski was systematically assaulted and hospitalised with concussion alongside another Solidarność leader, Mariusz Labentowicz. A 69-year-old peasant leader was also seriously injured.

Lech Wałęsa arrived in Bydgoszcz at 1am. Later he announced, "We shall respond resolutely, but calmly... someone's claws are getting too long, but we shall trim them... Not all the authorities are pigs. We wish to trust some of them." The last comment was interpreted as supportive of General Wojciech Jaruzelski, who had been named as Prime Minister on 11 February.

Solidarność assumed that this incident – the latest in a series of provocations – was led by Polish hardliners, backed by the Soviet leadership. Earlier that day a massive Warsaw Pact operation, Soyuz 81, had begun on Polish territory. There was now a majority on the Polish Politburo for a declaration of martial law, apparently only avoided by the threat of Jaruzelski's resignation.

Both the government and Solidarność had emphasised the need for dialogue, "Pole talking to Pole," and the Bydgoszcz incident was understood by everyone to be a break with that norm. Despite Solidarność's national leadership asking workers for restraint two-hour warning strikes shut down Bydgoszcz, Torun and other local towns. Posters of the beaten men lying on the ground, splattered with blood, went up across the country.

The 42-member National Commission, KKP, assembled in Bydgoszcz railway workers' social club on Monday 23 March to decide on Solidarność's response. On Wałęsa's proposal, and against more militant suggestions for an immediate general strike, a four-hour nationwide strike was called for Friday 27 March. If no agreement with the government was reached a general strike would be called for Tuesday 31 March. During the two days of debate Wałęsa walked out, implicitly threatening to resign if he did not get his way: if talks with the government on 25 March proved fruitless, the four-hour strike would start on Friday.

A set of demands included: punishment of those responsible for the Bydgoszcz incident; recognition of Wiejska Solidarność; abolition of a government diktat giving only half-pay to strikers; ending of all open cases against oppositionists arrested between 1976 and 1980. The government warned Solidarność that, "Without compromise, we shall plunge into chaos and may end in fraternal violence."

For safety, the 11-man national strike committee set up in the Lenin yard, Gdańsk, and the regional MKS strike committees were each based in large factories in their areas. Factories were policed by workers' defence guards wearing white and red armbands. Posters across the country declared, "We will not be smashed in the face."

At 8am on Friday 27 March the cranes stopped in Gdańsk. A massive banner opposing the police attack in Bydgoszcz hung from the gates of the Huta Warszawa steel plant. In Silesia the church bells rang and the pits stopped work. On television the screen was filled with a graphic which read, "The strike is on" (solidarność-strajk). The bulletin issued by the Ursus strike committee declared, "We are striking so that we might never again be beaten, jailed, or slandered, so that the police will pursue criminals, not trade unionists."

Solidarność exempted crucial services and hospital workers, for example, wore red and white armbands to show their support for the strike.

Wałęsa spoke at Warsaw factories declaring his trust in General Jaruzelski: "This is a uniform we can trust," and reiterating that the strike was not a challenge to the state or the Party's leading role.

At noon the factory sirens sounded the strike's end and the Polish working class went back to work. The strike had been a vast and magnificent display of the workers' power.

Solidarność had 9.5 million members, paying dues at 1% of their wages, from a total of 12.5 million eligible state workers. By this time Solidarność had 40,000 staff, seconded from their workplaces. The four hour strike was carried out with enormous discipline. Between 12 and 14 million workers took part. Over one million PZPR members defied instructions from their Party and struck.

Six hours after the strike ended the government started negotiations with the union. In the ornate Council of Ministers Palace in Warsaw the government finally admitted that the Bydgoszcz workers had been beaten in custody by police in civilian clothes. Andrzej Gwiazda insisted, "Now we want the names." Talks continued on Friday and the two sides agreed to reconvene on Monday.

The Party's 140-strong Central Committee met on Sunday 29 March against the background of continuing Soviet Bloc military exercises on Polish soil. Many worker-members spoke up against the violence and the hard-liner, Stefan Olszowski, threatened to resign after receiving much criticism. A metal factory foreman from southern Kielce declared, "We have to say it openly. Many people holding top Party posts want to keep them, without active commitment, at the expense of the working class, and they will use force." Janina Kostrzewska, a foreman in a computer factory in Wrocław said her local Party organisation participated in the strike "even though we were aware we were violating Party discipline. We read the events in Bydgoszcz as a clear violation of constitutional freedoms." She blamed the Party's top leaders for the strike, not the workers who struck.

The Central Committee lasted 18 hours, finally ending at 4am. It had not directly come to a conclusion about the next strike, due in two days time.

Wałęsa's close advisers and his link to the Church hierarchy, Professor Kukulowicz, pressed him to compromise and call the strike off; they said a general strike meant civil war.

Meanwhile many factories were being turned into fortresses. Food was brought in along with sleeping bags. At some plants petrol and chemicals were lined up to be used in self-defence. The young workers in the largest enterprises were the most determined; the activists were in a state of nervous determination, and everyone knew how serious the situation was.

When Gwiazda arrived for the final negotiations he did not sound hopeful. Nevertheless a deal was struck. Wałęsa had prevented other members of Solidarność's National Commission going to Warsaw and joining the negotiations. On Sunday evening he had telephoned Bogdan Lis and Zbigniew Bujak and insisted they stay in Gdańsk to prepare the strike, leaving negotiations in his hands. The discussions were mainly carried out by Wałęsa and a small group of his advisers, side-lining other Solidarność leaders. Behind closed doors the state threatened the union with using great violence.

At 7.30pm on Monday the television news showed the normally intransigent Andrzej Gwiazda — whom Wałęsa had persuaded to make the announcement, fearing for his own popularity and reputation — declaring that the strike had been suspended. Wałęsa stated that the union had got all it could, and he was "70% satisfied." However, what became known as the Warsaw Agreement had not won the Bydgoszcz demands. The farmers had not won the right to form a legal union. The clauses on political prisoners and strike pay were not specific.

This moment, the collapse of will and resolve, at a point when the working class was unified and determined and their state and Party enemies were in disarray, was the key event on the road to the military coup which came in December. Opinion polls taken in the run up to the strike suggested massive support for it. Timothy Garton Ash quotes a poll taken in the petrochemical-producing town of Płock which showed 79% for the general strike.

Lech Wałęsa came under intense criticism from voices inside the movement. Telex messages came in, many of which – especially from the best-organised areas – were angry and disappointed.

Solidarność's KKP met the next afternoon inside the Lenin Yard, Gdańsk. There were two issues debated: Was Wałęsa right to call the strike off for what was clear to many members was a poor and vague agreement? Was the decision taken in an acceptable, democratic way? Many members were more concerned about the way Wałęsa had behaved than the decision to call the strike off and much criticism was directed at Wałęsa's clique of advisers.

The debates were angry and emotion-filled. Eventually the meeting – which spilled over two days — ended having voted by 25 to four votes, with six abstentions, to confirm Wałęsa's decision to call off the strike. At that point it would have been difficult to reinstate the strike.

However Andrzej Celinski, a sociologist, whom Wałęsa relied on for organisational matters, was removed from his post as KKP secretary by a vote of 17 to 13 in a blow against Wałęsa. A message was sent to the meeting by Jan Rulewski, still hospitalised after the Bydgoszcz attack, denouncing the Warsaw Agreement as a sell-out. Roman Bartoszcze, the son of one of the men beaten at Bydgoszcz, complained that little had been achieved to win the farmers' demands.

Karol Modzelewski, co-author with Jacek Kuroń of the Open Letter to the Party, and now reactivated and in the role of Solidarność's Press Officer, resigned. Modzelewski stated, "From the point of view of union democracy it is intolerable to allow advisers to manipulate the situation... The final document, prepared by two advisers and I don't know who from the government side, was presented like a bombshell to the unprepared negotiators... This is a terribly dangerous situation." Modzelewski went further, discussing Wałęsa's role: "There is a king and a court around him and there is also a parliament... the king governs, with his court, and not the parliament. Why do I think this mechanism is a dangerous threat to the union? Because it will develop rapidly. Any attempt at criticism will be considered a scheme, a plot."

A few days after the meeting Andrzej Gwiazda, echoing Modzelewski, published an Open Letter to Wałęsa: "It was our fault, Lech, that union democracy was broken. I know we can both think of thousands of reasons why it happened, but I also know that *internal democracy within the union is a necessity*. The condition

73

in which it flourishes is full openness and a multi-directional flow of information. Its funeral is when criticism is crushed and union periodicals are censored. Each member of our union should have a right to criticise, even after a decision has been taken by the union... decisive influence is transferred to clerks and advisers who, uncontrolled, and without responsibility, have full freedom of manipulation."

Wałęsa replied: "You've written an Open Letter to me in which you remind me of our common struggle: free trade unions, the August strike, and Solidarność. I don't need to be reminded. I remember it well. I want the same now as then: that Poland will be Poland."

Of course opinion can change quickly and, in the days after the strike was called off, opinion polls showed a big majority of workers were now in favour of the decision to call the strike off. The mood of working-class self-confidence and militancy had been damaged, under-cut and wasted. Workers now remembered not their strength and solidarity, but how concerned and even frightened they had been.

On May 12 Wiejska Solidarność received legal sanction from the courts and gave the farmers the same rights for their union as industrial workers had won.

The Party's IX Congress

The leaders of various Eastern European Communist states were clearly concerned that Kania might lose control at the Party Congress. Czechoslovakian General Secretary Gustav Husak even publicly suggested the conference should be postponed. Just before the Congress Soviet Foreign Minister Andrei Gromyko arrived. Seemingly satisfied, the Soviets did not object to the Congress proceeding.

The pre-Congress elections in local and provincial Party organisations had seen a 50% turnover in personnel. Most of the 1964 delegates were between 35 and 45; 20% were workers; only 43 of the outgoing 142 full Central Committee members were elected as delegates. About 20% were Solidarność members.

The Torun "horizontal" opposition was a very marginal force at the Congress which met from 14-20 July.

The basic debate was between Kania and those pressing for a harder line against Solidarność.

Gierek and several of his supporters were expelled from the Party, blamed for creating the current crisis. Of the 200 newly elected Central Committee members only 16 had been full members of the previous CC. Of the 200, 41 were members of Solidarność. Kania was elected First Secretary with 1311 votes and in his new Politburo only three of the fifteen elected at the previous Congress were re-elected. Politically the Congress decided to continue trying to muddle through, shifting slightly towards a more hard-line position: commitment to Kania's cautious line of agreements with the workers' movement was to continue, but the Party was now opposed to making new concessions.

The workers' press

Two Solidarność newspapers were now being printed on state presses. *Jednosc* (Unity), edited by Leszek Dlouchy, a mechanic at the Szczecin shipyard, was launched in January 1981 and had a weekly circulation of 100,000 in north west Poland. In April *Tygodnik Solidarność* (Weekly Solidarity) began publication selling 500,000 each week. Both papers were between eight and sixteen pages, in tabloid format. The papers were published alongside daily bulletins, enterprise journals, radio cassette recordings, posters and leaflets.

Dlouchy, still in his twenties, led a team of seven workers producing *Jednosc*. Dlouchy commented, "We started as amateurs and are learning on the job. We are not professional journalists and therefore we do not have the ideological luggage of years of working for communist papers to unload."

Jednosc and *Tygodnik Solidarność* were both subjected to official censorship. *Jednosc* was considered the more radical; the moderate, Catholic oppositionist Tadeuz Mazowiecki edited *Tygodnik Solidarność*. It was impossible to buy *Tygodnik Solidarność* at a news kiosk. All the paper's print-run was distributed inside the factories. A factory with 10,000 workers would get 25 copies. Of *Jednosc*'s print-run 65,000 copies were sold in workplaces and 35,000 in kiosks.

KOR workers decided not to work with Mazowiecki and kept publishing *Robotnik*. In order to become more self-reliant a team of Solidarność printers went to Sweden on a printing course organised by the Swedish printworkers' union.

Most of the Solidarność regions produced weekly bulletins of between six and 12 pages in print runs of 20,000 copies. Larger regions such as Kraków and Wrocław had bulletins with print runs of 100,000. In Warsaw Solidarność was producing two daily bulletins with teams of messengers organised to distribute it to the largest factories.

In addition to the newspapers and bulletins Solidarność set up AS (Solidarity Agency), a news agency based in Warsaw and run by Helena Luczywo, a former *Robotnik* editor and KOR activist. Each week Luczywo's small team published a thick volume of news reports. Each page was typed and reduced, sometime carrying the equivalent of 200 pages of news and information. An edition would start with national news. A second section carried local reports. The third part contained the texts of official resolutions and statements. A fourth dealt with reports from experts and commissions; and the final section contained reproductions of Solidarność's plant and regional bulletins. Only 1,500 copies of each edition were published, at the relatively high price of 50 złotys (65 pence).

The NOWa samizdat press had now linked up with Solidarność to open 200 libraries providing material outside the official censorship system. The Warsaw office of Solidarność also provided a tape cassette service with tapes produced by Marek Chlebowicz, a worker at Polish state radio. Chlebowicz had been in Bydgoszcz in March 1981 when the local Solidarność leaders had been attacked. His tape of the incident was played on factory radio systems across the country. (Information: *Solidarity*, Denis MacShane)

The hunger marches

AS reported on the lavish lifestyle of the bureaucrats: Edward Gierek's villa was described to readers. The house was set in 4000 acres of parkland, with a billiard room, private cinema, and a dining room able to seat 40 guests. Waste and corruption were widespread with regular reports of food being wasted due to bureaucratic negligence. The situation for the working class was dire, demoralising, and getting worse.

Since the end of the Bydgoszcz crisis Solidarność had been trying to limit the use of strikes, the KKP agreeing not to strike unless the union's existence was threatened. Moreover Solidarność – remembering the times workers had been shot down on the streets — had always kept its action inside the enterprises.

Now, however, the economic crisis was looking vast and deep. In comparison with 1980 real wages in 1981 had fallen by 15%, the value of industrial production was down 18%, electric power by 6%, coal production by 16%, apartment completion by 15.5%.

The length of the average workweek had fallen by 8% while output per worker had fallen 12%. 30% of industrial plant capacity was unused from a lack of raw materials or equipment.

Foreign debt by the end of 1981 stood at $25.5bn and 3.2bn roubles to Eastern Bloc states. In 1981 exports had dropped 12% against 1980 and imports had fallen by 12% too.

Ration cards covered an increasing number of products, but these goods were not always available. Workers and their families spent enormous amounts of time searching for shops with food for sale; people left work to join queues. Wild-cat strikes broke out. Barter was increasingly used to obtain scarce foods.

The shortages of meat in the shops was partly caused by private farmers refusal to sell their animals to the state, especially in the second half of 1981. The farmers considered the prices – in Polish currency — they were being offered to be too low, against the increased costs of pesticides and fertilisers; they sold, instead, privately. According to official figures meat supply had fallen by 17% in the first six months of 1981. From August the meat ration was cut from 3.7kg of meat per month, to 3kg per month.

On the black market the exchange rate for dollars had gone from 120 złotys to the dollar in August 1980 to 250 to the dollar in the summer of 1981.

On 24 July to government announced that it would cut the meat ration by 20%

in August and September. The next day, on 25 July, 2000 people took to the streets in Kutno, central Poland. The protest was organised by the local MKS and the protesters carried empty pots and pans and signs reading, "We are tired of being hungry, tired of queuing". Bus drivers blocked traffic in the streets of Łódź and Piotrkow. Over the next week scores of similar protests took place across Poland.

In Łódź, a town of 800,000 people, 50,000 workers took to the streets on 30 July, and again the march was organised by leading Solidarność activists. The main bulk of the protest was made up of women and children; the demonstration was quiet and sombre with groups of women singing hymns; men hung about the edges, protecting the procession. Łódź was a textile town where, of the rationed goods, only butter and flour were available. The women worked long hours in sweatshop conditions and now there was no washing powder to clean their work clothes.

On 3-4 August a motorcade organised by Mazowsze MKS, at the initiative of militant transport workers, snaked through Warsaw to protest against ration cuts and shortages. The police stopped the convoy of trucks, cars and busses as it attempted to pass the Party's headquarters, at which point the parade stopped for 48 hours, blocking the roads in central Warsaw. The state's right to control the streets was now being contested.

Mieczysław Rakowski for the government met Wałęsa on 3 August, the first meeting since 23 June. Rakowski bitterly complained that Solidarność's strikes had caused the food crisis. The official press, under Stefan Olszowski, aggressively worked the same theme. Solidarność threatened a printworkers' strike unless the relentless anti-union campaign in the press ended. In fact the strike took place on 19-20 August. It cut newspaper production from nine million papers per day to two million, with two-thirds of all printers taking part.

By organising the local hunger protests Solidarność members were assuming the roles more often associated with activists of a workers' political party; they were the tribunes of the people. But who would solve the food crisis and economic crisis? That crisis required governmental-level action. For the workers to solve the crisis in their own interests they required a workers' government based on their own power in the factories.

In a country where every single working class action quickly became political, directed against the Stalinist state, the Polish bureaucrats and Soviet imperialism could not tolerate the existence of Solidarność. They found these hunger marches acutely alarming.

Zbigniew Bujak remarked that Solidarność found itself like, "a union of seamen on a sinking ship." But Solidarność was not willing to take control of the ship. That created a certain opportunity for the Party, and opinion polls began to show a significant minority favouring "drastic measures": in June one poll showed 78% positive support for Solidarność, while 87% gave the Party a poor rating, but 31% approved of "strong political leadership, discipline and obedience" as the only solution to the crisis.

Solidarność's unwillingness to take power was creating a basis of support for the counter-revolution.

Solidarność's Congress

All the union's leaders concluded that the union must begin to take a more active role in political affairs.

Solidarność demanded complete information about the country's internal and external trade figures and access to government stores. They demanded the right to check and direct the distribution of meat and other products in short supply. That was the question of workers' control of distribution.

The question of control over industrial production was more complex, and contested. From March 1981 a network of committees in large workplaces had been spontaneously set up, alongside Solidarność and even against the wishes of the main leaders, committed to "self-government" inside the enterprises. By July workers' organisations in 3,000 factories, shipyards and mines were linked up. In practice the movement insisted on managers being selected on the basis of competence, rather than Party alignment, in heavy industry.

Minimal though this was, it was a direct threat to the *nomenklatura* system. The quarter of a million strong Party-state ruling class felt its jobs and privileges were directly under threat. And, of course, the central problem had not been addressed: if state power remained in the hands of the Party overall planning decisions, inter-relationships between factories, economic priorities and planning would still remain under the control of the hostile, anti-working class bureaucratic ruling class.

Solidarność was dividing down ideological lines, between pragmatists, led by Wałęsa, who believed in the necessity of compromise with the regime, and radicals. But the division between the two tendencies was also unclear and unstable; and "radical" meant refusing to compromise with the regime rather than advocates of working-class power in society.

Solidarność had been renewing its leadership. The Party's bosses waited to see what Solidarność's Congress would decide, while issuing a clear warning. Kania, closing a Central Committee Plenum on 3 September said, "Our enemies say the authorities will surely not introduce a state of emergency in Poland. [But the government] will resort to every means which may be necessary."

The first stage of Solidarność's Congress took place on 5-10 September in Gdańsk. 896 delegates represented 9.5 million workers. Half the delegates were under 33 years old, 43% worked in industry or mining, 86% were married and only 8% were women. The majority were skilled workers (50% had a car and a telephone compared to 17% country-wide). A big majority (over 80%) had been active in the Polish state's fake unions prior to the creation of Solidarność.

Less that 10% were members of the PZPR and 9% were members of the Stalinist youth organisation.

In the first sessions no programme was agreed, but a statement of priorities was drafted including demands for controls over production, distribution and pricing, and abolition of the *nomenklatura* system. The most contentious decision was to send a message to the workers of Eastern European and Soviet workers. Mild and short the message included: "We support those among you who have decided to follow the difficult struggle for a free trade union movement. We have the firm hope that our representatives will be able to meet each other."

The Soviet news agency, TASS, denounced extremists who had turned the Congress into "anti-socialist and anti-Soviet bacchanalia." Responding, Lech Wałęsa repeated that the union did not want power but control over the authorities so that they would serve the people. The Polish Party leaders knew that the Russians' patience was running out.

Solidarność was – dangerously – leaving unorganised by themselves large groups of the population: students, farmers, retired workers. Many of these people could have found a place in a genuine workers' party. Wałęsa was resolutely set against the formation of a new party although discussions began to take place about the creation of workers' political education groups.

Later, in November, Jacek Kuroń's apartment was raided when activists were gathering to found an organisation called Clubs for a Self-governing Republic. The Ministry of Internal Affairs described the police action as necessary to prevent the formation of an illegal organisation, a political party, which was being founded to engage in anti-state activities.

Between 11 and 25 September 13 working groups met to draft sections of Solidarność's programme. The clearest division between moderates and radicals took place in the 11th working group charged with formulating the union's desired relationship between the union and the Party-state. One wing thought that reforms such as abolishing the Party's monopoly on nominations for the Sejm (Stalinist semi-parliament) and creating a second chamber would be adequate. Fundamentalists wanted to explicitly reject the 'leading role of the Party'. The union's advisers, Tadeusz Mazowiecki and the human rights lawyer Wladyslaw Sila-Nowicki, argued strongly on the side of the pragmatists.

Two reports were published by the 11th group, with the radicals demanding multi-party democracy, "social ownership" of the means of production to replace the Party's monopoly of economic authority, and to remove Party organisation from the workplaces.

The second part of the Solidarność Congress began on 26 September. The free-wheeling, noisy Congress developed an anti-intellectualism, the product of frustration with the advisers' moderation. None of the well-known advisers were elected to the new National Commission.

The state media was banned from the Congress to protect the union from misrepresentation in the official media.

KOR announced its dissolution on the grounds that its work was now being carried out by the union.

Elections took place for the Chair of the National Commission. Wałęsa was opposed by three other candidates: Andrzej Gwiazda from Gdańsk; Jan Rulewski, the militant from Bydgoszcz; and Marian Jurczyk from Szczecin, leader of the August 1980 shipyard strike. Wałęsa, who did not bother to campaign for votes, received 55%, Jurczyk got 25% and the other two less than 10% each. Wałęsa's victory was clear. Nevertheless perhaps 40% of the Congress voted for a more militant leadership than Wałęsa.

The Congress agreed a new National Commission, comprising the 38 Chairs of Solidarność's regional boards and 69 members elected on the basis of the number of members in each region. So Upper Silesia (Katowice) had 11 representatives, Mazowsze (Warsaw) and Lower Silesia (Wrocław) had 8 each, Kraków had 6, down to three mini-regions which had no representation. A Presidium to the National Commission was also formed, with 11 of 12 candidates designated by Wałęsa being elected.

Solidarność's programme was voted on. Divided into eight sections and 37 theses the introduction included this statement: "In the face of national tragedy, Solidarność must no longer restrict itself to expectations and to exerting pressure on the authorities to keep obligations stemming from the agreements... The union considers it its fundamental duty to take every possible step... to save the country from misery, apathy and self-destruction. There is not other way than by reforming the state and the economy on the basis of democracy."

The union was being drawn into politics in a way that implied collaboration with the regime, even against the immediate interests of the Polish working class. So, for example, although Solidarność demanded the abolition of *nomenklatura* system and "public [depoliticised] control over the Government's anti-crisis decisions" it also now accepted the need for massive price rises and the resolution by special courts of all labour disputes.

13 of the 37 theses were headed, "The Self-governing republic" in which reforms to authoritarian rule were proposed, rather than a multi-party democracy and the election of a constituent assembly. The final text was a compromise between reformers and fundamentalists. At the end of the Congress a delegate

who was also a Party member said that the ideas that had been agreed which would be particularly objectionable to the authorities were: separation of economic control from political control; public control of the means of production; introduction of Solidarność television and radio stations; abolition of the state monopoly of foreign trade.

The Party works towards crushing the workers' movement

The Price Commission announced the first major price increases on 3 October when cigarettes, tobacco and matches doubled in price. Solidarność threatened strikes and began 50 hours of negotiations with the government demanding an equal say over economic decision making, which was rejected by the government.

At the Party's Central Committee plenum (16-18 October) Kania received a barrage of criticism. He resigned as First Secretary on the third day and his resignation was approved by 104 votes to 79. Olszowski wanted the job but General Jaruzelski, already Prime Minister and commander of the armed forces, was elected by 180 to 4 votes. It was unprecedented in Eastern Europe that a serving army officer should be leader of the Party or government.

Solidarność's leadership interpreted the change in leadership as meaning little would change and the Party would still seek a negotiated settlement. Kania and Jaruselski both had similar backgrounds, having risen under Gierek; both had been understood to oppose Olszowski's calls for a crackdown.

Jaruzelski, Prime Minister since February 1981 had put a number of military officers into political roles. For example, after the Bydgoszcz crisis in March and the resignation of the chair of the Provincial Council, Jaruzelski appointed a general to the vacancy. When the workers at the Polish airline, LOT, elected their new director Jaruzelski intervened and appointed an air force commander instead, causing the LOT workers to strike.

As the Party renewed itself in the run up to its July Congress a number of active military officers were elected to various posts.

In September the government launched a campaign under the slogan "Order and Security" which embedded army personnel in police patrols. Jaruzelski extended army conscripts' two-year service period by two months. At this point Solidarność should have intervened on behalf of the conscripts, championing their rights, but it failed to do so. Squads of soldiers began to be used to intervene in villages and towns, allegedly to improve local administration.

Soldiers doing military service were asked to volunteer to work in the mines (apparently 7500 did so).

Police applying a new censorship law arrested Solidarność members selling union publications in Katowice and those broadcasting union news from a van in Wrocław. Solidarność's leaders debated the situation at length on 25-26 October and called a one-hour national strike on 28 October. The union was showing discontent with the government but also trying to assert control over a series of spiralling strike actions occurring across the country. Jaruzelski declared the strike a failure, although Solidarność assessed their action as well supported. The union appealed to local organisations to end local strikes. Jaruzelski asked the Sejm to ban strikes, but the rigged parliament resisted and only made an appeal for strikes to end.

While planning the coup that would come in December Jaruzelski simultaneously offered discussions on a coalition government, or Front of National Accord. The idea had been first raised in December 1980 in the columns of *Polityka*. On 4 November Jaruzelski met Lech Wałęsa and Archbishop Glemp, the Primate of Poland, to discuss ways of overcoming the crisis and the possibility of forming a Front of National Accord. This was a snare for the union.

The government pursued their tactic. Rakowski said, effectively, in a newspaper interview, that the Party was willing to share power: "The era of commands is gone forever, not only in the economy, but in politics." A different message was coming from hardliner Olszowski, however, who said the Party would never agree to a coalition government.

In November and December a new wave of student occupations began. One of the colleges occupied was the Warsaw Fire-Fighting school. On 2 December the occupation was violently broken by large numbers of ZOMO police. The next day Solidarność's leadership met in Radom. Wałęsa declared, "Confrontation is inevitable and will take place. Let us abandon all illusions. They have been thumbing their noses at us."

After the ZOMO attack on the school there were signs that some of the police wanted union rights. 'The Founding Committee of the Trade Union of the Civil Militia' objected to the raid, declaring that, "The militia was formed to protect the interests of society as a whole, not those of the ruling minority." Solidarność made no attempt to organise dissenters inside the police or the armed forces, and so to disorganise the repressive machinery of the state.

Wojciech Jaruzelski (1923-2014)

December 1981: the coup

The deals Solidarność had struck had accepted the Party-state and the union had agreed not to challenge the Party's right to rule. The Solidarność revolution of 1980-1 was a self-limiting revolution, and by making half a revolution Solidarność was to prove, negatively, the need for working class militants to develop their own political organisation with the perspective of taking power. The Stalinist Party-state could accept no open opposition to single-party, authoritarian rule.

After August 1980 there were two powers in Poland. One would overthrow the other. Wałęsa had believed he could work with Jaruzelski, but Wałęsa had engaged in hopeful, wishful thinking. He had disorientated and politically disarmed the millions that followed him.

On the night of Saturday 12 and Sunday 13 December 1981, General Jaruzelski had the Council of State pass legislation to introduce martial law. There was one vote against, Ryszard Reiff of the state's Catholic organisation, PAX. Jaruzelski — a man whom Wałęsa had loudly proclaimed to the working class as someone who could be trusted — established the Military Council of National Salvation, comprising of 21 military officers, a move which also had the effect of side-lining the PZPR.

At the same time as a legal framework for military rule was being legislated Jaruzelski had most of the Solidarność leadership arrested in their Gdańsk hotel rooms. Thousands of local Solidarność leaders, student activists, farmers' union leaders and former KOR activists were also detained. Telephone lines were cut off, a curfew and harsh travel restrictions were imposed, meetings were banned and Solidarność offices seized, schools and universities were closed, and military rule was imposed on the media and many workplaces. Technically, from the regime's immediate point of view, the coup was extremely successful.

A six day working week was declared and military rule in a workplace meant workers who refused to follow orders could face a court martial. Price rises meant real wages were cut by 20%.

Archbishop Glemp broadcast an appeal for the workers not to fight back.

Utterly unprepared – Solidarność had no definite plan to respond to a coup, and had not seen the crackdown coming – the movement had lost almost all of its central leaders.

Jaruzelski addressed the nation at 6am on Sunday 13 December to attempt to justify his actions. He said that Poland was "on the edge of an abyss." He needed to save the "dying economy" saying, "Strikes, the readiness to strike, actions of protest have become a norm of life." The state had mobilised and used as much force as necessary to smash the opposition.

Later, after the fall of Stalinism in Eastern Europe, a Polish Parliamentary commission suggested that around 90 people had been killed in the initial phases of martial law. In the week after the coup there were scores of work sit-ins, occupations and stoppages. On 16 December, at the Wujek pit in Silesia, nine miners were killed as workers fought the ZOMO para-military police with metal pipes and crow-bars. Armoured cars and tanks were on the streets.

Without key leaders workers' opposition was uneven and patchy. The Piast miners occupied their pit, underground, for three weeks. When they finally surfaced they were amazed to find the government in control; they had expected Poland to have been shut down by strikes.

The Soviets and other leaders of the Eastern Bloc welcomed the coup. The West, however, was taken by surprise. The US imposed sanctions including the suspension of $100m of emergency food aid and President Ronald Reagan accused the USSR of putting pressure on the Poles to smash the opposition. The Western Europeans agreed that the Russian leadership were partly responsible but did not see the sense in imposing economic sanctions on Poland.

Martial law was to last until June 1983, although a general amnesty was not granted until 1986. Conditions of life in Poland meant 700,000 emigrated to the West from 1981-89. A number of aircraft were even hijacked from Poland to Germany by those trying to leave.

In the period December 1981 to May 1986 alone, 1600 illegal dissenting organisations were smashed by the police and 1200 duplicating machines confiscated. None the less, roughly 1350 different samizdat publications were issued, among them *Tygodnik Mazowsze*, compiled with the assistance of former KOR members and sometimes reaching a circulation of 40,000.

Even under conditions of extreme repression the Stalinist state could not silence the authentic voice of working-class opposition and the willingness to fight for freedom and workers' liberty.

Riot police outside a Solidarność office, December 1981

In the initial phase of Martial Law over 90 people were killed and most of Solidarność's leaders were arrested. Key factories and industries were placed under military control. Crowds in Warsaw shouted "Gestapo!" at the military

Tanks on Polish streets. Martial law was introduced on 13 December 1981 and only lifted in July 1983

APPENDICES

From the Polish coup to the present day

A brief summary, by Stan Crooke

Ongoing repression of Solidarność throughout the 1980s – despite the lifting of martial law in 1983 and the official amnesty granted to its victims in 1986 – was accompanied by a series of economic reforms, similar to those pursued by Gorbachev in the Soviet Union from 1985 onwards.

The ruling Stalinist elite began to privatise state property in the name of 'market socialism'. Non-core economic operations, which were often more profitable than the centralised major industries, were sold off to managers and Party officials ("nomenklatura privatisations").

At the same time state-owned enterprises were nominally opened up to market forces. They were to be independent units of production, self-financing and self-managed (i.e. by managers, not the workers). In theory, their financial performance would determine their profitability and rates of pay.

But given that control of investment in industry remained centralised in the hands of the state, and was thereby subject to all the failures inherent in bureaucratic top-down 'planning', the independence of enterprises remained largely illusory.

These reforms did nothing to resolves Poland's ongoing and deepening economic crisis.

Inefficiencies at the level of the individual enterprise increased. Shortages in shops became more frequent and more widespread. Waiting lists for consumer goods lengthened. More and more human labour and raw materials were wasted on the production of substandard goods.

Insofar as the economy functioned at all, it did so on the basis of bribery and barter between individuals and enterprises. In other words, the defining features of the Stalinist economy remained intact.

In the late 1980s the intensifying economic crisis resulted in a new wave of working-class strikes and protests. Increases in the price of food of up to 40% in February of 1988 triggered strikes across Poland.

93

Gdańsk shipyard workers struck in early May but returned to work within a week. Strikes by miners in the July Manifesto Mine quickly spread to other mines. This, in turn, encouraged strikes in other industries and a renewed strike by Gdańsk shipyard workers.

The strikes were only a shadow of the industrial insurgency of 1980. But they were sufficient to make the PZPR realise that piecemeal reform of the Stalinist command-economy was not viable.

The economic crisis had not been resolved. There was the risk of a rebirth of working-class militancy. To resolve the former and prevent the latter, the PZPR turned to the leaders of Solidarność.

Despite having being driven underground – the union had been formally banned in October 1982 – Solidarność structures had been maintained in a weakened form throughout the decade. At the same time, the more compromising elements in it had become increasingly dominant.

State repression had disproportionately impacted on the more militant and more radical elements in Solidarność. Sometimes for personal reasons, sometimes for political reasons, Solidarność had also suffered a succession of splits.

The absence of mechanisms for democratic accountability under conditions of state repression had also allowed Wałęsa to restructure Solidarność's leading bodies at will – the Temporary Council of NSZZ Solidarność (1986), the National Executive Committee of NSZZ Solidarność (1987), the Citizens Committee (1988), and the Solidarność Citizens Committee (1989).

By the end of the decade control of the much weakened Solidarność organisation was firmly entrenched in the hands of Wałęsa, his supporters, and his pro-free-market intellectual allies. Modzelewski contemptuously referred to them as "the republic of buddies."

In August the PZPR responded to the strikes triggered by its hike in food prices by calling for talks with Solidarność. Wałęsa took up the offer and met with the PZPR Minister of Internal Affairs five days later. The next day all strikes were called off and Wałęsa prepared for further talks with the PZPR.

Those talks took place in Warsaw from February to April the following year: the Round Table Talks. The name itself summed up how far the Solidarność leadership had travelled in the course of the decade.

These were not talks in which union leaders and the PZPR confronted each other on opposite sides of the table, with their negotiations broadcast live to striking workers.

But these were private talks in which Solidarność and PZPR leaders sat around the same table, shared a common purpose, and discussed a comprise outcome with the assistance of representatives of the OPZZ Stalinist fake trade union federation, 'independent authorities' (i.e. Stalinist-run front organisations) and two priests.

And that despite the fact that the PZPR had banned Solidarność, imprisoned thousands of its members and killed nearly a hundred of them, while the OPZZ, a creation of the PZPR dating from 1984, had been the recipient of all Solidarność land, property and equipment seized by the PZPR during martial law.

Unsurprisingly, Wałęsa's readiness to lead Solidarność into such talks triggered a further split in Solidarność. The Fighting Solidarność faction – committed to confrontation rather than conciliation with the regime, but also politically committed to Polish nationalism rather than working-class socialism – walked out of the organisation.

The upshot of the talks was: legalisation of Solidarność, creation of the post of President, creation of the Senate as a second chamber (in addition to the Sejm) and the holding of what came to be called 'semi-free' elections, in which all seats in the Senate and 35% of seats in the Sejm would be contested. The other 65% of seats in the Sejm were reserved for the PZPR.

Solidarność emerged from illegality and quickly grew to some 1.5 million members – far fewer than prior to its outlawing, but still a potential major social force. But whether, and how, that potential might be realised depended on the politics of the organisation's leadership.

Their politics was clear from the public statements issued in the run-up to the 'semi-free' elections of June: support for the introduction of the 'free market', and support for a moratorium on strikes.

Solidarność contested the elections under the name of the Solidarność Citizens Committee, winning all 161 contested seats in the Sejm and 99 out of 100 seats in the Senate. Neither Solidarność nor the PZPR had expected such a level of success.

But the turnout in the June elections had been a reflection of demobilisation and demoralisation: 62% in the first round, and just 26% in the second round.

After the tragedy of the failure of the Solidarność leadership to resolve the dual power situation in favour of working-class rule in 1980-1981 came the farce of its willingness to promote the particularly brutal 'shock therapy' transition to capitalism launched in 1990.

With the support of Solidarność parliamentarians, the newly elected Sejm elected Jaruzelski as President. Solidarność itself formed the new government, headed by members of Wałęsa's "republic of buddies": Mazowiecki was Prime Minister and Balcerowicz the Deputy Prime Minister and Minister of Finance. The new government also included PZPR parliamentarians.

The Balcerowicz Programme of 'shock therapy', drawn up with the assistance and support of the World Bank and the IMF, was put into effect in January of 1990. State subsidies and public spending were slashed.

The newly created Ministry of Privatisation carried out the function embodied in its name. Poland was opened up to global competition. Unemployment rocketed and wages slumped.

The main beneficiaries of the mass privatisations were members of the old Stalinist elite, alongside of a layer of the Solidarność "republic of buddies". But for many of Solidarność's rank-and-file activists of the 1980s 'shock therapy' meant unemployment and poverty – and the need to organise resistance to 'their own' government.

A new wave of strikes was organised by Solidarność activists (grouped together in the Network (Siec)) and ex-Solidarność activists (who founded Solidarność '80). There were 305 strikes in 1991, 6,322 in 1992, and 7,443 in 1993.

Coal and copper miners, transport workers, teachers and other public sector workers played the leading role in the strikes. In late 1992 Solidarność called a national strike against increases in the cost of living and all mines in Upper Silesia were shut down by a general strike.

In early 1993 300,000 workers across Poland struck for a month. In the spring Warsaw was virtually shut down by a Solidarność-organised two-day strike.

Opposition to the role played by Solidarność parliamentarians also found expression within Solidarność itself. Conflict between its different factions intensified. Wałęsa talked of "war at the top" as dissatisfaction mounted with his failure to galvanise opposition to government policies.

In the autumn of 1990 Wałęsa 'banned' the *Gazeta Wyborcza* newspaper from using the Solidarność logo. The paper had been launched after the Round Table Talks as the Solidarność election campaign paper.

Its slogan had been "Nie ma wolności bez Solidarności" ("There is no freedom without Solidarność"). But for Wałęsa freedom did not extend to freedom to criticise Solidarność parliamentarians, and Wałęsa himself.

Wałęsa stood down from office in Solidarność after his election as Polish President in 1990. But the 1991 Solidarność congress 'rebelled' by refusing to elect his 'appointee' as his successor.

In the spring of 1993 the wave of popular protest resulted in the Sejm passing a motion of no confidence in the government and the calling of new elections.

The SLD (the post-Stalinist successor to the PZPR) and the PSL (Polish Peasant Party, based on farmers' opposition to the impact of 'shock therapy') won two thirds of the seats. Candidates standing under the Solidarność banner picked up less than the 5% of the vote needed to win seats in the Sejm.

Two years later Wałęsa was defeated by the SLD candidate in the 1995 presidential election. The SLD-PSL coalition government largely continued the policies implemented by its predecessor, even if in not so aggressive a form.

But working-class opposition to its policies collapsed. Levels of unionisation were in decline, and demoralisation was widespread. There were never more than 42 strikes a year under the coalition, with a maximum of 42,000 strikers in any year.

Closely linked to the SLD – given that both were post-Stalinist successor organisations descended from the same nomenklatura – the OPZZ now repeated the role played by the Solidarność leadership in the early 1990s.

It stifled working-class unrest to allow for the pursuit of anti-working-class policies by the SLD-PSL government.

Dissatisfaction with the record of the SLD-PSL coalition, scandal-mongering agitation around the Stalinist past of leading figures in the SDL, and hypocritical denunciations of the demobilising role played by the OPZZ provided the opportunity for a new foray into electoral politics under the Solidarność banner.

In 1996 the AWS (Solidarność Electoral Alliance) was created, an alliance of some 40 Catholic and right-wing organisations which laid claim to the Solidarność heritage and included some of the union's current and former leaders.

In the following year's parliamentary elections the AWS campaigned as defenders of workers' rights against SDL-PSL attacks and as champions of traditional Polish values (defined as Catholicism, patriotism and the family) which were supposedly at risk form the SDL.

But the AWS's supposed commitment to the defence of workers rights certainly did not include support for working-class self-activity. Marian Krzaklewski, Solidarność chairperson and a co-founder of the AWS, opposed calls for a general strike during the election campaign on the basis that the best general strike would be a vote for the AWS in the election.

The AWS won 34% of the vote and 201 seats in the Sejm. It formed a coalition government with the neo-liberal UW (Freedom Union).

The new government included former Solidarność leader Jerzy Buzek as Prime Minister, Balcerowicz (who had switched to the UW since his last term of office) as Deputy Prime Minister and Finance Minister, and Solidarność leader in Łódź, Janusz Tomaszewski, as Interior Minister.

A new round of privatisations was unleashed by the AWS-UP coalition government. This second wave, following on from that of 1990, introduced the market into public services, privatised pensions, and restructured welfare services and local government.

The health sector bore the brunt of the attacks. AWS-UP 'reforms' introduced private health insurance, privatised sectors of the health service, and fragmented the previously nationally organised health service. Spending cuts resulted in hospitals being shut down and a 30% cut in staffing levels.

Doctors, nurses and midwives staged demonstrations against the "reform" throughout 1999. The following year, after implementation of the "reforms", nurses demonstrated, went on strike, squatted in government ministries, and staged hunger strikes in support of their demands for better pay and working conditions.

After around 25,000 nurses demonstrated in Warsaw in June, the government agreed to a pay rise. But by August 90% of nurses still had not had their rates of pay increased. This triggered a fresh round of strikes and occupations of public buildings.

The response of Tomaszewski as Interior Minister was to authorise the use of rubber bullets against protesting health workers, and the use of anti-terrorist police against nurses' occupations.

The AWS and UP paid the price for their record in the power in the 2001 elections. In a virtual re-run of the 1993 elections the former won 5.5% of the vote, and the latter 3%. Both parties lost all representation in the Sejm – the hurdle for electoral alliances had been increased in 1997 to 8%.

The AWS lingered on to contest the 2002 regional assembly elections, when it secured just 3.4% of the vote. Two new right-wing parties emerged from the demise of the AWS: PO (Civic Platform) and PiS (Law and Justice).

The 2001 elections had been won by the SLD, which formed a coalition government with the UP (Labour Union, a small social-democratic party). But all subsequent elections for the Sejm (2005, 2007, 2011, 2015 and 2019) were won either by the PO (traditional right-wing) or the PiS (hard right-wing and populist).

After 2001 Solidarność focused primarily on its role as a trade union and on attempting to make good the damage it had suffered through its association with the AWS. Public opinion polling found that 70% of negative attitudes towards Solidarność in the early 2000s were based on its association with the AWS and the latter's record in power.

This was despite the fact that many – or, according to some reports, the majority – of the strikes against the AWS-UP coalition's policies had been organised by Solidarność members.

Solidarność found itself operating in a hostile environment. The post-1989 economic transformation of Poland had created an unfavourable terrain for union recruitment.

De-industrialisation swept away the industries and enterprises in which Solidarność had been based, replacing them by service industries, micro-enterprises and the gig economy. 96% of Polish firms now employ less than ten workers, and 40% of Polish workers are employed by them.

The union also faced 'competition' from the FZZ trade union federation (founded in 2002) and the larger OPZZ federation, neither of which were tainted by Solidarność's links with the governments of 1989 and 1997.

Solidarność's membership had slumped – from ten million in 1980 to 1.5 million after legalisation, with further losses triggered during and after the 1989 and 1997 governments. Between 2001 and 2005 Solidarność lost a third of its membership. By 2008 its membership was less than 700,000.

This was in the context of an overall fall in the level of unionisation in Poland, down to around 12% today, one of the lowest rates in Europe. Unions have only a minimal presence in the private sector and multinationals. Solidarność and the OPZZ both claim memberships of 500,000, while the FZZ claims a membership of around 400,000.

And although Solidarność withdrew from overt electoral interventions after the demise of the AWS, it has continued to show political sympathies for the AWS-successor organisation PiS.

Janusz Sniadek, Solidarność chairperson from 2002 to 2010, had close ties with the PiS leader Jaroslaw Kaczynski, allowed Solidarność meetings to be used to build support for the PiS, and stood as a PiS candidate in the 2011 elections.

Sniadek's successor as Solidarność chairperson, Piotr Duda, promised a fresh start, free of political alignments on the part of the union. But his own politics place him firmly in the orbit of the PiS.

In 2018 he allowed the former Gdańsk shipyard rooms where the historic Gdańsk Agreements were signed to be used by the ultra-nationalist ONR ("Death to the Enemies of the Homeland", "We Will Defend the Holy Faith") for a rally which called for an "ethnically homogenous" Poland.

In 2019, by contrast, he criticised the European Solidarność Centre in Warsaw, which houses the history of Solidarność, for renting out a room to an LGBT organisation: "This is not the kind of freedom we fought for. Solidarność was born under the cross."

Duda has also been noticeably more energetic and militant in challenging the record of PO governments than in challenging the record of PiS governments, even calling for a general strike to bring down the last PO government (2011-2015) of Donald Tusk.

(Wałęsa responded by calling on Tusk to "treat them (Solidarność) with police batons." In 2019 he launched a petition to stop Solidarność calling itself Solidarność, on the basis of the union's ties to the PiS. But Wałęsa's hostility to the PiS is personal rather than political. He and PiS leader Kaczynski hate each other.)

By contrast, on the eve of a major teachers' strike in 2019 Solidarność broke ranks with the OPPZ and FZZ by signing up to accept a pay offer by the PiS government of 9.6%. The two other unions continued to demand and strike for 30%.

The pay deal with the government was signed by the head of the teachers' section in Solidarność, Ryszard Prokska — a PiS member and local government representative. He promised "consequences" for Solidarność members who went on strike anyway.

All this is far removed from the Solidarność of 1980.

Solidarność at that time was a mass movement of militant struggle, capable of overthrowing the Stalinist regime. Today it has lost 95% of its membership, struggles for its survival in the face of competition from the OPZZ and FZZ, and is in the political slipstream of right-wing populism.

Its fatal mistake in 1980/81 was its adherence to the idea of a "self-limiting revolution". The political opponents whom it confronted in a situation of dual power placed no such restraints on their actions.

First they crushed Solidarność under martial law. Then they used its leadership to push through the 'shock therapy' and repeated waves of privatisation whereby the Stalinist command economy in Poland came to be replaced by free-market capitalism.

None of this was historically inevitable. Of all the anti-Stalinist protests which exploded in Eastern Europe during the 1980s, Solidarność was the only one which took the form of a new specifically working-class organisation.

But it was an organisation of which the leadership lacked the perspective and drive to replace the Stalinist sham 'workers state' by a genuine workers state based on working-class democratic rule.

There is no disputing the heroism of the struggles of Solidarność in the 1980s. But, some four decades later, the Polish working class continues to pay the price for its failure to take those struggles to their logical conclusion.

As we were saying...

A Open letter...

Socialist Organiser, 13 September 1980

Socialist Organiser, the newspaper published by a forerunner of the Alliance for Workers' Liberty as the Polish workers fought for a new independent movement, attempted to rally the British workers' movement in support of Solidarność.

The struggle was complicated because some of the most prominent advocates for Solidarność in Britain were the right-wing newspapers, Tory politicians and right-wing trade union leaders. They had their own agenda, of course, which was to use Solidarność to discredit socialism which they identified with the Polish Stalinist state.

At the same time the official mainstream of the trade union movement had long-established, friendly, "fraternal" ties to the Polish Stalinists, and formal links with their state-run fake unions. British trade union bureaucrats regularly went on official visits to Poland, allowing the Polish Stalinists to make propaganda from the pleasant holidays enjoyed by British union officials. The British union leaders' acceptance of the Polish police state "unions" helped legitimise the Polish "unions" inside Poland to the benefit of the Stalinists.

And the problem was compounded because some of the more militant labour movement leaders and rank and file activists in Britain were Stalinists, or influenced by Stalinism. Cynical British Stalinists used the right-wing support for Solidarność to make a case against the new, mass Polish workers' movement.

Socialist Organiser attempted to untangle the mess, advocating support for Solidarność, whilst opposing the hypocrisy of the right.

We promoted a socialism based on working-class militancy, democracy and opposition to Stalinism.

This article appeared in *Socialist Organiser* (issue 25), 13 September 1980. Frank Chapple was a notorious, vicious, right-winger who ran the electricians' union, the EETPU.

An open letter to Frank Chapple

M r Chapple,

You protested noisily against the decision of the TUC to send a delegation to Poland as guests of the strikebreaking police-state 'trade unions' of that country. You have called on the TUC to support Polish workers in their struggle.

You advocate free trade unionism independent of the state — for Poland — and you seem to think that the TUC would have been best employed helping the Polish workers create such unions instead of hobnobbing with the bureaucrats of Poland's sham unions.

Excellent! What you said on this matter needed to be said. That it was said most vehemently by the one figure in the British labour movement most odious to socialists and militant trade unionists is a terrible verdict on the state of that movement's official leadership.

Every thinking worker in Britain, everyone who has ever known what it is to give or receive basic class solidarity in a strike, every worker who would revolt against a police tyranny over the British working class, ardently sympathised with and wanted to help the workers of Poland. He or she felt betrayed and dirtied by the bumbling and spineless bureaucrats of the TUC who were so eager to be the guests of those who run Poland's 'company unions' for the Polish and Russian Stalinists.

They are people without honour and without principle who shamed the labour movement and themselves by their fawning on the anti-working class Polish Stalinists. Just like they do by their docility before the Tory offensive against the British working class.

But who are you, Mr Chapple? You are a professional anti-socialist and anti-communist, eager to pretend that the police state in Poland is socialism and that socialism is thereby discredited. You are a man initially installed as a leader of his own union by a High Court judge, instead of by election, a man widely denounced as a scab by his own union's members — and with good cause.

You run the nearest thing to a 'union police state' in Britain. You have more than once played the role for the capitalists of Britain that those that the TUC was going to visit in Poland always do for the bureaucrats there.

Of course, Britain is not a police state, and despite your own tin-pot despotism

103

in the EETPU, despite your readiness to call in the state and its courts to arbitrate in the affairs of the labour movement, the EETPU is a genuine workers' organisation, qualitatively different from the police state 'trade unions' of Poland. Even you, Chapple, sometimes have to represent the interests of your members, and even to fight for them.

In the last analysis it is this that determines that you, despite what you are, came out on the right side in this question. You are part — a malignant part, but still a part — of a real working-class movement, whereas the Polish 'trade unions' are designed to prevent a real Polish workers' movement from emerging.

The problem, Chapple, is that your support taints the cause you say you support. Militants in Britain who know you for what you are in the British labour movement and in the fight against the bosses here may thereby become confused about who is who and what is what in Poland right now.

The TUC discredits only itself; you, by your championing of them, threaten to discredit the Polish strikers in the eyes of a lot of good working class militants, especially those who mistakenly believe that the system in Poland is some sort of 'socialism'.

The *Morning Star*, the newspaper of the Communist Party of Great Britain, which tried to whitewash Gierek and the other Polish tyrants, eagerly seized the chance to tell those working-class militants who read it just how many of the enemies of socialism and of working class militancy in this country were 'supporters' of the workers' struggle in Poland, ranging, as they did, from yourself to the *Sun* and *Daily Mail* newspapers.

In fact, Chapple, you don't really support the Polish workers at all. No doubt you do rejoice at the troubles of the Polish Stalinists. But you are a liar if you say you support what the Polish workers were fighting for. Or in any case you oppose in Britain most of the demands the workers in Poland fought for.

Let us look at their demands.

• Do you support free trade unions, independent of the state and the managers? The Polish workers do.

But you run autocratically the least democratic union in this country. It is only thanks to the intervention of the state within the workers' movement that you, Chapple, are where you are today. Rather than independence from the state, you have slavishly sought interference by the courts to maintain your grip. You accept the Employment Act (with the state financing of postal ballots which would tie the unions closer to the state) and want to work it for the Tories.

• Do you support the right to strike, the safety of strikers and all those who support them? The Polish workers do.

You support the legal right to strike, of course. But you have publicly scabbed on many strikes. In the 1968 grading dispute in Scotland, your members when they demonstrated, had to wear masks to protect themselves from expulsion from the union.

Trade unionists wearing masks to protect themselves from victimisation: that's one of the most striking images of the recent struggles for democratic trade unions in Britain. They wore the masks to protect themselves from you and your machine, Mr Chapple.

• Do you support the right of strike committees to get access to the media to publicise their demands. The Polish workers do.

But in your case, Chapple, it would be more appropriate to ask first, do you support strike committees? Such committees would be the death-knell of your own stranglehold on the EETPU.

As for access of workers to television and radio to put forward their demands honestly, this would cut directly across your own privileged access to the bosses' media, with which you usually collaborate to slander and vilify the militants of our class.

• Do you support open democratic debate, the ending of state secrecy, and the access by workers to all the facts and figures of economic and social life? The Polish workers do.

But what about open democratic debate within your own union for a start? Chapple, the internal goings-on in your union are probably some of the closest guarded secrets in this country — especially from EETPU members! And Chapple, think how the bosses, the civil service mandarins, and all those other parasites who rule our lives, parasites with whom you work hand in glove, would fight bitterly against any move to break down their monopoly of information and the mystique of 'expertise' with which they try to blind and confuse us.

• Do you support the sliding scale of wages — wage increases to compensate for the rise in the cost of living? The Polish workers do.

Chapple, your record of strike breaking, your sabotage of even the most minimal struggles of workers who are determined not to bear the brunt of the bosses' crazy system, is answer enough to that question.

• Do you support the Polish workers' demand that the privileges of the police, and the secret police, should be abolished? That special shops for the bureaucrats should be eliminated?

But, Chapple, you are one of the most vociferous advocates of 'law and order' and security, almost always on the wrong side when cops smash up picket lines. You do not criticise the multitude of anti-working class special police and espionage organisations which the capitalists find essential to maintain their class rule in this country and to frame up militants, revolutionaries, and those fighting for

105

the freedom of the Irish people.

As for the special shops — have you ever denounced the exclusive shops of London, whose prices are so astronomical that no working class family could ever afford even to contemplate shopping there? No doubt on your salary such problems seem a mere trifle?

- Do you support early retirement, at fifty years of age for women and fifty-five for men? The Polish workers do.

- Do you support improved working conditions, medical services and facilities which workers need?

Chapple, we have never heard you protest angrily, let alone do anything about the dismantling of the welfare state, the closing of hospitals and schools. Nor have you ever protested against the miserable conditions that millions of our class slave under in small non-union sweatshops, constantly raided by the police in search of 'illegal immigrants', nor have we heard you protest against speedups, undermanning, and the capricious and petty foremen who have sold out their class and do the bosses' bidding on the shopfloor.

- Do you support increases in nursery provisions to meet the needs of working mothers, and the extension of maternity leave for women to three years on full pay? The Polish workers do.

Since when has your union made a stand on the rights of working-class women, let alone the right of women to work, and not be sacked first as a matter of course, when profits are bad for the bosses?

Finally, Chapple, the Polish workers are not fighting for the return of industry to private ownership. All reports tell us that socialised industry is accepted as the basis of a democratic alternative to Stalinism, that is, inescapably, as the basis of a democratic working-class system. In other words, the Polish workers are in agreement with the programme of the socialisation of industry under workers' control, which socialists fight for in this country and you fight bitterly against.

These, Chapple, are the demands that the Gdańsk workers fought for. The 21 demands of the Inter-Factory Committee of Gdańsk are firmly on the terrain of our class's age-long fight against the capitalists and of the decades-long struggle to overthrow the ruling Stalinist bureaucracies.

Your support of the Polish workers, Chapple, is only so much hot air and bluff. A mass movement for the same programme in this country would sound the death knell of your rule in the EETPU. In British working class politics you fight against those who stand for the programme the Polish workers fought for — and you use all the arts and tricks of the turned-around, inside out 'Stalinist' that you are.

The programme of the Polish workers and the victory (as yet not consolidated) they have won, should inspire the British labour movement to move into action against theTories, to fight for what the Poles demanded. The day we do move, Mr Chapple, will see you lined up squarely with the Giereks and Brezhnevs of Britain — against us, and against the programme of the Polish workers.

Jim Denham, Angus McDougall, George Makin, Frank McGuirk (T&GWU shop stewards, BL Longbridge), Steve Griffiths (AUEW shop steward, Rover Solihull), Frank Henderson (NUSMW deputy senior steward, BL Longbridge).

A letter to Scargill

During the great British miners' strike of 1984-5 the Sunday Mirror newspaper attempted to use remarks apparently made by Lech Wałęsa against the miners' leader Arthur Scargill, in order to undermine the strike movement. Scargill was a militant, fighting the class struggle in Britain, but he was a Stalinist and a friend of the Polish regime and opposed to Solidarność.

This article is from Socialist Organiser (issue 200) 11 October 1984

Arthur Scargill, Lech Wałęsa: militants in distorting mirrors

Poland's government has been sending scab coal to Britain [exporting coal which undercut the British miners' strike action], while Solidarność has declared support for the NUM. But some people on the Left are using a *Sunday Mirror* report that Lech Wałęsa attacked Arthur Scargill to justify their hostility to Solidarność. John O'Mahony discusses the issues.

The Sunday Mirror some weeks ago printed an account of an interview with Solidarność leader Lech Wałęsa in which Wałęsa appeared to side with Margaret Thatcher against the miners. The Sunday Mirror headlined the piece "Why Scargill is wrong — by Lech".

Quite a lot of Solidarność's friends in Britain were shocked and its opponents, semi-opponents and outright enemies — of whom there are a very large number in the British labour movement — seized on the article. It is cited again and again by labour movement activists to condemn Solidarność.

What did Wałęsa say? That is less clear than the *Sunday Mirror's* headline suggests, but I will quote the Sunday Mirror.

After an opening sentence by the interviewer (or the sub-editor in the Sunday Mirror office), "Lech Wałęsa has condemned violent tactics in Britain's pit strike", Wałęsa is quoted as saying: "The miners should fight, but with common sense — not with destruction. Because whatever is destroyed has to be rebuilt.

"I disagree with any violence. The workers should demand the maximum, but not at the risk of bankrupting the employer."

The interviewer (or sub-editor) introduces another quote like this: "Wałęsa had a message for Arthur Scargill". This is the "message": "Go into the matter carefully and assess how much one can squeeze. But without destroying.

"It is forbidden that ambition takes precedence over hope.

"Trade union activists should lock away their ambitions.

"They should calculate on their computers how much they can get but, I repeat, not at the sake [sic] of destroying the structure."

The journalist then says that Wałęsa expressed "much respect" for Margaret Thatcher and quotes him: "With such a wise and brave woman, Britain will find a solution to the strike."

I have cited all the direct quotes attributed to Wałęsa about the miners' strike and about Thatcher.

Now it is by no means impossible that Wałęsa would condemn trade union "violence" or produce this rather vapid philosophising on realistic trade union-ism. And he may well, because of her strident rhetoric against the USSR, Poland's overlord, think Margaret Thatcher is wise and brave.

These views would identify him as right wing or soft left if he operated in the British labour movement.

But for many on the left it isn't a matter of disagreeing with Wałęsa. They question Solidarność's right to exist. They seize on things like the Sunday Mirror article to support the grotesque idea that the entire Polish labour movement is reactionary or "counter-revolutionary". They adopt a soft, tolerant or even friend-ly attitude to the Jaruzelski regime which has been trying to destroy the Polish independent trade union.

The refusal of the *Morning Star* to print a paid advert or a letter condemning Jaruzelski for sending scab coal to Britain is one measure of the state of the British labour movement on this question: the *Morning Star* was clearly confident that it would not suffer for this implicit solidarising with Jaruzelski against the miners.

In an interview in last week's *Socialist Organiser*, Tony Benn MP responded to a question about Polish scab coal by asking: "But what about Wałęsa supporting Thatcher?" And Benn would not sign the letter to the *Morning Star*.

Lech Wałęsa may — or he may not, as we shall see — have given the Sunday Mirror the comments which were used against the miners. We know for certain that Jaruzelski has sent scab coal to help Thatcher, increasing by three times Poland's exports of coal to Britain since the miners' strike began.

So Wałęsa may have made a few Neil Kinnock-like comments to the *Sunday Mirror* criticising miners' violence and Arthur Scargill's ambition. The conclusion does not follow that Jaruzelski — who gives Thatcher scab coal — was therefore justified in banning the Polish trade unions and attempting to destroy them!

Eric Heffer MP was right when he said in *Socialist Organiser* two weeks ago: "The entire movement in this country should have given Solidarność total support. Free trade unions [in Poland] would not have allowed coal to come in now".

The same message came in a broadcast from Solidarność miners in Silesia: "The underground Provisional Co-ordinating Committee of Silesian miners sends you fraternal greetings and our support and solidarity for your struggle for the right to work.

"We will do everything possible to support your struggle, including in action. The protest we have sent to the Polish government and Parliament is an initial measure taken in support of your struggle".

In *Socialist Organiser* we have also published this message from the Inter-Factory Network of Solidarność in the Warsaw area: "The slave labour of the Polish miners serves to break the resistance of the British miners.

"British miners! In the prevailing conditions of terror the Polish workers' movement is at present not in a position to undertake protest actions. But you may be certain that we are in solidarity with you".

David Jastrzebski, president of the Solidarność committee in Upper Silesia, has sent this letter "to the striking miners of Great Britain": "Our organisation sends you full support for your struggle. We are full of admiration for your stance and your unfailing willingness to struggle. We believe you will achieve your goals.

"Neither the British government's mounted police charges nor its truncheon blows, any more than the Polish junta's tanks or rifle fire, can break our common will to struggle for a better future for the working class.

"We appeal to all members of Solidarność to support your struggle. Only the international struggle of the mass of workers can decide our fate".

To Arthur Scargill personally Jastrzebski wrote: "Allow me to send you the expression of my support and my enthusiasm. For many weeks you have represented the interests of your trade union with dignity.

"At the same time I ask you to consider our own difficult situation — activity which is clandestine and under totalitarian threats — which means that there are many things we cannot resolve rapidly, often for security reasons.

"In the coming weeks we will send you greetings from other organisations [of Solidarność] which support your struggle.

"I wish you the best, and above all victory. I ask you to send our greetings to all British miners and our best wishes.

"Personally, I am convinced that thanks to the attitude of your trade union victory is within your grasp".

In any case, to repeat, whatever Wałęsa might say against 'violence' or against Arthur Scargill is irrelevant to the right of the Polish workers' movement to exist. Our duty to defend its right to exist cannot depend on the opinions of one of its leaders — or of Solidarność itself.

There are many in our own unions and in the Labour Party who condemn the miners and would like to cut Arthur Scargill's throat. We denounce them of course — and we organise against them. Only a suicidal maniac would conclude that trade unions, because they are led by Eric Hammond of the EEPTU or John Lyons or David Basnett, forfeit their right to exist. Yet that is the underlying idea of those who pounce on Wałęsa's interview and say "We told you so" about Solidarność.

Wałęsa is quoted saying things against a section of the British labour movement — therefore it is right for the Stalinist dictatorship to destroy the Polish labour movement? It is preposterous.

Solidarność is a great working class mass movement, which had ten million members when it was outlawed in December 1981, 18 months after coming into being.

It is a unique movement. Never before have independent trade unions emerged in any Stalinist state.

Such a movement will span an immense range of opinions as ours does. The 11 million strong British labour movement has Labour Party right wingers, Liberals, SDPers, Tories, racists, some fascists and... Stalinist supporters of foreign anti-working class dictatorships like Jaruzelski's.

Our movement — unlike Solidarność — is led by a quite distinct caste of materially privileged bureaucrats. We propose to change it politically, reconstruct it, democratise it — not help the 'reforming' Tories put it down.

Nor can it make any difference that industry is nationalised in Poland and Jaruzelski can perhaps claim to be defending nationalised property (though Solidarność did not threaten to attack it).

For socialists, nationalisation is a means to an end, not the end: the end is socialism. The liberation of the working class from capitalist exploitation and from state tyranny.

Nationalisation is necessary for socialism, but it is not socialism, nor the only condition for socialism!

In the Stalinist states nationalised property is controlled by privileged bureaucrats by means of a state tyranny over the people which is unparalleled in history.

The Polish labour movement was born in conflict with a state tyranny much of whose power over society comes from the state's control of the means of production.

Suppose that movement were, in reaction against Stalinism, to advocate restoring capitalism — though Solidarność did nothing of the sort — even that could not lead working class socialists to side with a Jaruzelski standing for nationalisation and "socialism" against "counter-revolution".

Real socialism, which liberates the working class, and therefore society, from both exploitation and state tyranny, can only be created by the working class itself, acting in freedom.

The Polish labour movement — even were it making terrible errors — is a great deal more important to socialism than is nationalised property under the control of a tyrannical bureaucracy, parasitic on the labour of the workers, and holding them in a police-state vice.

The right of the labour movement to live, its ability to grow and to discuss its experience and its programme for society — nothing in Poland, or in any of the Stalinist states, has a greater value than that, for socialists who base themselves on the first letter of the socialist alphabet, formulated by Karl Marx as follows:

"The emancipation of the working class must be the act of the workers themselves".

In fact Solidarność did not propose to restore capitalism.

In fact Wałęsa is in no way the equivalent of our own tame right-wing trade union leaders — he is in working class history the equivalent of figures like Tom Mann, Jim Larkin, AJ Cook or... Arthur Scargill.

And in fact it is by no means certain that Wałęsa said what the *Sunday Mirror* puts in his mouth. In so far as I can find out, an interview was in fact given by Wałęsa to Robert Eringer who is an American or Canadian freelance journalist.

However, the comments quoted from Wałęsa do not justify or license the *Sunday Mirror*'s headline. The quotes are all just snippets, too short for any context to be discernable.

It is not indicated to what questions Wałęsa was responding. You have to take it on trust that Wałęsa is not being quoted out of context by the interviewer, or by the office sub-editor who gave the article its final shape.

What would Wałęsa — who was an underground free trade union activist and a victimised and persecuted militant for years before the strikes of 1980 — say in response to questions from a militant miner who told him the facts?

Worse than that. The impression created by the interview is achieved by the headline and by the reporter's or sub-editor's comments inserted before the quotes from Wałęsa. You depend on these inserts for much of the sense of what Wałęsa is made to seem to be saying.

Right at the beginning it is the *Sunday Mirror* which says Lech Wałęsa condemns "violent tactics in Britain's pit strike". Wałęsa, as quoted, doesn't say that.

112

The *Sunday Mirror* says he is condemning the miners, but unless you know what question he is responding to, or the broader context of what is quoted, you have only the Sunday Mirror's word for it. For all you can know for sure from what is quoted, Wałęsa might even have just been talking generally and talking too in the certain knowledge that the Polish secret police were recording every word for possible use against him.

Take the question about assessing "how much one can squeeze" and about "ambition". It is the reporter who says it is "a message for Arthur Scargill". Apart from the "framing" first sentence all you have there is Wałęsa philosophising in general terms about sensible trade unionism.

The reporter or the sub-editor has clearly pruned, cut, selected and processed the "raw material" provided by Wałęsa. Yet the quotes are presented as continuous and breaks aren't indicated. For example, that is plainly what happened in the following passage. The first sentence obviously doesn't go with what follows, though they are put into a single paragraph:

"I disagree with any violence. The workers should demand the maximum, but not at the risk of bankrupting the employer."

So the *Sunday Mirror* article is not reliable, trustworthy reporting. A careful reading of the article shows that it has little hard, indisputably authentic information about what Wałęsa thinks of the miners' strike.

The article has many of the marks of something "processed" in the newspaper office and slanted to make a pretty routine interview topical and interesting by linking it to current news in Britain and in a piquant and unexpected way.

Wałęsa may have expressed such views and it may be that he admires Mrs Thatcher for her hostility to the USSR. But we have no reason to take the Sunday Mirror's word for it.

Many oppositionists in East Europe and the USSR — and probably Wałęsa — do have a friendly attitude to people like Thatcher and US President Reagan because they are strident enemies of the Kremlin. Their attitude is: my enemy's enemy is my friend.

For a Wałęsa that is short-sighted and based on a fundamental misunderstanding.

Thatcher and Reagan may say kind things about Solidarność because it is opposed to the Kremlin, but they are hostile to their own 'Solidarnośćs' and use the law and the police against them.

Just like the Kremlin bureaucrats, in fact, who try to use the labour movements in the West while stamping on the workers in their own domain.

Oppositionists in the East who favour the West are merely a mirror image of those workers in capitalist society who adopt a friendly attitude to the Stalinist

113

A palm-sized samizdat edition of the Polish-language Trotskyist publication, Imprekor, carried a translation of our Open Letter to Scargill from Socialist Organiser *200, 11 October 1984*

dictatorships. Our Stalinists and quasi-Stalinists see only everything negative in the West and think nationalised property is working class socialism in the East. So they favour the East.

The oppositionists in the East see that there is personal freedom in the West, the right of the workers to organise trade unions and political parties and to publish more or less what they like. That, in contrast to the arbitrary state tyranny in the Stalinist states there is the rule of law. So, they idealise the West.

Both views are one-sided and false: indeed, the Easterners' view is probably less one-sided and less false than that of the Stalinist workers in the West.

It is no small difference, after all, that in the advanced capitalist countries we have won the right — through centuries of struggle — to organise freely, while everywhere in the East the workers are subjected to a savage repression which nips in the bud every stirring of independent working class activity and jails or kills its organisers.

It is easy to understand why the Eastern oppositionists and, especially, the

Socialist Organiser

John O'MAHONY

JEDNOŚĆ ROBOTNIKÓW WSCHODU I ZACHODU

DLACZEGO POWINNIŚMY POPIERAĆ "SOLIDARNOŚĆ"
NIEZALEŻNIE OD TEGO, JAK PRASA Z FLEET STREET
USIŁUJE WYKORZYSTAĆ LECHA WAŁĘSĘ PRZECIWKO GÓRNIKOM

Londyńska gazeta "Sunday Mirror" opublikowała kilka tygodni temu relację z rozmowy dziennikarza Roberta Eringera z przywódcą "Solidarności" Lechem Wałęsą, w której ten ostatni został przedstawiony jako człowiek opowiadający się po stronie Margaret Thatcher a przeciw strajkującym górnikom. Opatrzyła reportaż Eringera tytułem: "Dlaczego Scargill nie ma racji - mówi Lech". Wśród wielu przyjaciół "Solidarności" w Wielkiej Brytanii wywołało to szok, podczas gdy jej oponenci, półoponenci i zdeklarowani przeciwnicy - których jest bardzo wielu w brytyjskim ruchu robotniczym - rzucili się na artykuł Eringera. Jest on cytowany w tę i z powrotem

przez wielu działaczy ruchu robotniczego, potępiających "Solidarność".

Co mianowicie powiedział Wałęsa? Z artykułu Eringera nie wynika to zbyt jasno wbrew temu, co sugeruje nagłówek, jakim go opatrzył "Sunday Mirror". Zacytujmy więc artykuł. Po zdaniu wprowadzającym, sformułowanym następująco przez dziennikarza (lub redaktora w biurze "Sunday Mirror"): "Lech Wałęsa potępił stosowanie taktyki przemocy podczas strajku w brytyjskich kopalniach", przytacza się wypowiedzi Wałęsy: "Górnicy powinni walczyć, ale z rozsądkiem - nie zaś w sposób niszczycielski. Bowiem co się zniszczy trzeba odbudować. Nie zgadzam się z jakimkolwiek

38

The John O'Mahony (Sean Matgamna) Open Letter to Scargill, as translated in the Polish-language Inprekor

fighters for free trade unions in a Stalinist state, might idealise the advanced capitalist countries. They shouldn't, of course.

We who live in a country like Britain know how hollowed-out much of the freedom and democracy is, where the multi-millionaires rule, backed by an anti-working class state. We know that the workers are savagely exploited under capitalism and have to fight every inch of the way, as the miners are having to fight now.

If Wałęsa were really to attack the miners and Scargill, he would only be paralleling the attitude Scargill has adopted Solidarność. In fact it is highly improbable that Wałęsa would not protest if the Tory government banned the TUC and the NUM, and jailed thousands of militants.

According to the *Sunday Mirror* Wałęsa attacked miners' "violence." But large sections of the British labour movement, including Scargill, have attacked Solidarność's very right to exist. They failed even to protest when it was banned, and they told British workers that Jaruzelski represented socialism in Poland and

115